RED BOOK
Wide Range Readers

Phyllis Flowerdew

Oliver & Boyd

Illustrated by J. Crawford Fraser

OLIVER & BOYD
Longman House
Burnt Mill
Harlow
Essex CM20 2JE
An Imprint of Longman Group UK Ltd

First published 1980
Ninth impression 1992

© Phyllis Flowerdew 1980
All rights reserved. No part of this publication may be
reproduced, stored in a retrieval system, or transmitted in
any form or by any means, electronic, mechanical,
photocopying, recording, or otherwise, without either the prior
written permission of the Publishers or a licence permitting
restricted copying issued by the Copyright Licensing Agency
Ltd, 90 Tottenham Court Raod, London W1P 9HE.

ISBN 0 05 003192 9

Printed in Hong Kong
WP/09

The Publisher's policy is to use paper manufactured form
sustainable forests.

Preface

There are six Wide Range Readers Red Books. They can be used alone or with Wide Range Readers Blue and Green, with which they are parallel. The controlled vocabulary and graded sentence structure makes them suitable for children with the following reading ages:

7 to $7\frac{1}{2}$ years	– Book 1
$7\frac{1}{2}$ to 8 years	– Book 2
8 to $8\frac{1}{2}$ years	– Book 3
$8\frac{1}{2}$ to 9 years	– Book 4
9 to 10 years	– Book 5
10 to 11+ years	– Book 6

The success of Wide Range Blue and Green Books has been proved through the years, and the author hopes that the addition of the Red series will bring pleasure to teachers and children.

Contents

The Monastery 5
Small Stories – 1 19
Karli and Kit 21
The Story of Bub 26
Chess Stories 37
A Page of Riddles 44
The Wreck of the *Strathmore* 45
Hiawatha 57
The Camp 59
Sleeping Heroes 69
Little Boy Lost 73
Silly Stories 88
Evonne 89
Small Stories – 2 102
Jet Flight 105
Juliane in the Jungle 117
News of Dinosaurs and Others 129
A Stitch in the Air 131
Once Upon a Time 139
Johnny Appleseed 149
Old Cars 153
To the North 155
Canals 169

The Monastery

Little Lobsang cried. He was cold and hungry. He was wrapped in a rug and tied on the back of his yak, but the bitter wind cut through him like a knife. He wanted to go home, though he scarcely remembered what home was like. Nor did he remember the early weeks of the journey. His whole world now had become the mountains.

These were the Himalayas, the highest in the world. They towered over him. They enfolded him. They froze him. They filled him with awe and fear. The snow lay deep and white, and sometimes when the sun shone on it, it glistened with a thousand tiny sparkling lights, or it hurt his eyes with a blinding, dazzling glare.

Lobsang cried. He also coughed, a racking cough that tore painfully at his chest. This, no doubt, had been brought on by nights spent in the open curled up in the snow with Kalsang and Pemba and Dolkar and Diki. Kalsang was his mother, and Dolkar his sister. Pemba was his aunt, and Diki was her little daughter.

Today there was a mountain pass to cross. Nearly every day there was a mountain pass to cross. Kalsang walked in front, stumbling, plodding on, leading the yak. Dolkar had grown quiet these days, and she still looked back with longing to their home in a village not far from Lhasa, the capital of Tibet. She remembered standing at the door of the house, and gazing at the Potala Palace in the distance, and looking at the haze that hung above the city. The haze was caused by butter lamps and prayer stoves and yak-dung fires. The Potala Palace was very old. It was the winter home of His Holiness the Dalai Lama, the god-king, and it was built upon a mighty rock. It was built on the rock and in the rock, so that it seemed to be part of the rock itself.

But now there was fighting in Lhasa. The Dalai Lama had gone across the mountains to India, and many of his people had followed him.

Deep in her own thoughts, Dolkar trudged along behind her mother, with Diki close beside her. Diki still bubbled over at times with chatter and fun, though at other times she wept with cold and hunger. Pemba came last, leading the pony. The pony had been weak and ill, but now it seemed to be better again. Upwards they walked, upwards, upwards.

Suddenly a patch of snow gave way at the side of the pony. The pony slid down on to a ledge that jutted out above a deep crevasse.

"Help me! Help me!" cried Pemba. By a miracle, she was still on firm ground, and was still grasping the leading rein.

"Here, Dolkar, hold the yak," gasped Kalsang, and she went to Pemba's side and helped her to pull on the rein. The tough, little, frightened pony struggled and struggled to clamber up the steep, snowy rocks. Its four legs seemed to shoot out in all directions, and clouds of snow flew up around it. Its frantic efforts began to loosen the packs on its back, and two of the bundles fell far, far below.

Dolkar stared in horror. She was terribly afraid that, instead of Kalsang and Pemba pulling the pony up, the pony would pull them down. She held the yak tightly and sent up a prayer. Diki clutched at her mother's skirts and pulled backwards with all her might.

Perhaps it was Dolkar's prayer. Perhaps it was the tiny bit of extra strength given by Diki, but next moment the pony was safely on firm ground again, and Kalsang and Pemba and Diki had all fallen backwards into the snow. They scrambled to their feet and brushed the pony down and re-fixed its load. Kalsang muttered a prayer of thankfulness to the gods of the mountains, but Pemba wailed,

"We've lost two bundles. It's some of our food, and some of the food for the animals."

"Oh never mind!" murmured Kalsang. "*We* are all safe. We could so easily have fallen down the crevasse to our deaths."

"And the pony's safe," said Diki. "Good little pony." She patted it and put her cold cheek against its face.

Lobsang cried more loudly. He was facing the other way and he could not see his mother at all.

"Mummy, Mummy!" he screamed. Then a cough choked him, and he coughed and coughed and could not stop. Kalsang went quickly to his side and untied him and sat him up until the coughing had passed.

"When we get over the mountain pass, we'll make some tea," she said soothingly. "We have a little bundle of sticks that we collected yesterday on the lower ground where there was hardly any snow. We'll make a fire and melt some snow and make tea. You try to sleep a bit

now." She made him as comfortable as she could and tied him firmly on the yak again. Then the two families plodded on, upwards and upwards.

Sometimes the track round the mountain side was so narrow that they walked in fear of their lives. One slip of a foot, and someone would easily go hurtling down, down to death. Sometimes the track was wider but became a sheet of ice. Then the two women had to spread some of their precious rugs on it to help the animals to get a foothold.

At last the mountain pass was behind them. The animals were panting. Their breath rose in white clouds above them. Their shaggy coats were wet.

Pemba made a hollow in the snow and somehow managed to get a fire going. She boiled the water and broke off a piece of tea-brick, now becoming very small. She made the tea and mixed a little butter in it. Thankfully Dolkar and Diki drank. Kalsang cradled Lobsang in her arms and he sipped weakly at the tea.

"I'll nurse him while you drink yours, Mother," said Dolkar a little later. So she held her little brother, while Kalsang and Pemba drank their tea together and talked quietly.

"I hope we can reach a village tonight, Pemba," said Kalsang. "We shall soon have to buy some more food. Besides, I'm worried about Lobsang. He ought not to sleep in the open any more."

"The villages are so far from each other," replied Pemba. "Perhaps we can sometimes find monasteries, and seek shelter in them."

"If we can climb up to them," said Kalsang. There were more monasteries in Tibet than anywhere else in the world, but most of them were built in most difficult places. They clung to sheer rocks. They brooded over mighty valleys. They reached towards heaven itself.

"Mother," put in Dolkar quietly. "I think Lobsang is ill." He lay in her arms, flushed and very hot. His eyes were closed, and for one terrible moment Kalsang thought he was dead.

"We *must* get help for him today," she whispered. Then he opened his eyes and began chattering in a feverish way.

"My yak wants to go with those other yaks," he said.

"What other yaks?" asked Dolkar.

"Those, over there – that long, long string of yaks and ponies – hundreds of them going round the mountain."

Everyone looked up at the mountains, but no one could see any yaks.

"Where, Lobsang? Where?" demanded Diki. He waved his arm feebly towards the track they had still to follow.

"Hundreds of yaks – with His Holiness," he said. They all looked again – Kalsang, Dolkar and Diki. They looked for the Dalai Lama, their god-king. They looked but they saw only the lonely, wild beauty of the Himalayas. There were no yaks.

"You're dreaming," laughed Diki, but Kalsang's heart felt, for a moment, strangely lifted. Little Lobsang had seen a vision, she was sure. He had seen a vision, and it was good.

. . . . .

If Kalsang's spirits were lifted by a drink of butter tea, and by Lobsang's feverish chatter, they did not remain high for long. As the day wore on, with all its hardships, she became more and more worried about the little boy. He lay in a burning fever, coughing pitifully, and often scarcely able to draw breath. Sometimes the jogging of the yak seemed more than he could bear, and Kalsang and Pemba took it in turns to carry him. He would not try to eat anything, and Dolkar was often in tears for him.

"*When* shall we come to a village where we can get medicine for him?" she kept asking.

"I don't know. We must have faith," said Kalsang. Her own faith was almost forgotten now in her anxiety. Home and happiness had been left far, far behind, and it seemed as if Lobsang at least, might never reach India.

"Look! A monastery!" cried Diki at last. "We'd better take Lobsang there." The building stood up against the sky like a fortress on a great rock. Golden, bell-shaped towers rose from the flat roof, and a line of tattered prayer flags fluttered in the wind.

By the time the families came within reach of it, they were almost at the end of their strength. Dolkar was leading the pony now, and Diki was taking a turn riding on the yak. Lobsang was in his mother's arms, and Kalsang and Pemba were stumbling forward, keeping the monastery in sight. There it was, not so far ahead, but high, high above them. There it was, against the cold, blue sky; and leading up to it was a flight of steps cut in the solid rock, and going in a zig-zag line up and up and up.

"We can't do it," murmured Kalsang. "We'll never do it."

"We must," said Pemba.

Then help came. Two young, strong monks appeared from a rock close by, leading two sure-footed horses that had been up and down the steps a hundred times before.

"We were expecting you," said the taller of the monks. Kalsang and Pemba looked a little surprised. Then they thought,

"They must have seen us coming in the distance."

"We know the little boy is very ill," said the other monk. "Our abbot-doctor has herbal medicines ready to ease his breathing and reduce the fever." Kalsang and Pemba gasped. "We know the little boy is very ill," the monk had said. How could he know he was ill? How could he have known that there was a little boy at all?

Soon the two women and Lobsang were riding up the zig-zag steps on the horses' backs. It was certainly not a comfortable ride, but they were filled with thankfulness and awe. Behind them came the monks leading the pony and the yak, and carrying Dolkar and Diki.

A boy monk met them at the entrance to the courtyard. He was no older than Dolkar, but he led the pony and the yak away to be unloaded and fed. An old monk opened the door of the monastery before anyone had knocked.

"We were expecting you," he said kindly. "Our abbot-doctor will see the little boy at once." He led the two families across the great hall, where their footsteps echoed in the silence. Dolkar noticed the red, wooden pillars painted with shining patterns in yellow and blue. She noticed the long gallery hung with banners, something like those in the temple at home. The air was heavy with the smell of butter lamps, hundreds of them glowing in the gloom. In the place of honour was a huge statue of Buddha, and all round the walls were pictures showing scenes from his life.

Another monk appeared and led Pemba and Diki away to a guest room, while the older monk took Kalsang and Lobsang up a flight of stairs. He meant Dolkar to go with Pemba, but she clutched at her mother's skirt and would not leave her side. Lobsang lay quite still in Kalsang's arms and she wondered fearfully whether he were already beyond help. In a moment she and Dolkar were taken before the abbot-doctor, and Kalsang realised with a pang that she had no white good-luck scarf to give to him. His room was very dim, and had its own small statues and gold and silver bowls and butter lamps.

The abbot-doctor was an old, old man with a straggly grey beard. He dipped his fingers in a tiny dish of liquid and spread it gently over Lobsang's forehead. He gave him sips of herbal medicine and he muttered prayers. He said,

"I will send up prayers for the little boy during the night and again at dawn, and a monk will bring him medicine again, soon."

"Thank you," murmured Kalsang with her hands together and her head bowed.

There were four beds in the guest room. They were like raised wooden platforms with thick cushions and blankets on them. There was also a table, and a small cupboard painted with pictures of birds and flowers. A monk brought a meal of tsampa (beaten rice) and cheese, and a bucket of hot butter tea, which he ladled into drinking bowls. After the meal Diki curled up on a bed and was asleep in a moment.

"You try to sleep too, Pemba," said Kalsang. "I'll wake you if I need you." Dolkar wanted to sit up and help to look after Lobsang, but after a while, she too dropped back on the cushions and fell asleep. It was the first warm, comfortable night any of them had had since leaving home. They felt as if they were sleeping on clouds.

It was early in the evening and Kalsang listened to the low chanting of the monks. She tucked Lobsang up in bed and then she sat beside him and turned her small prayer wheel and sent her prayers up to heaven. All the prayers were set prayers that Tibetan children learned by heart. People did not pray for favours for themselves. Even Kalsang could not pray for her little son to be healed. Only a senior monk could pray on her behalf.

Soon the chanting of the monks ended, and silence fell upon the monastery. A single butter lamp burned in the guest room and cast weird shadows on the walls. A monk brought Kalsang a bowl of hot soup, and a little later he returned with medicine from the abbot-doctor. He gazed at Lobsang, now tossing feverishly in the bed, and fear gripped Kalsang's heart, for she knew the monk was thinking how ill the little boy was.

"Don't worry," he said gently, as if reading her thoughts, and he began to talk to her, to cheer her a little.

"Have you heard any news of His Holiness?" he asked. Kalsang shook her head.

"No, but today in his illness, my little boy said that he could see him going round the mountain with a long, long string of yaks and ponies – hundreds of them, he said."

"He spoke truly," nodded the monk. "His Holiness passed along the track on which you came yourselves. It was many days ago, and we pray that he is now in India, in safety."

"Tell me," said Kalsang suddenly. "How did you know that we were coming here with Lobsang so ill?"

"The abbot-doctor saw you and the child in a dream," he replied.

Then he slipped silently away, and Kalsang watched the shadows and the flickering lamp. She touched Lobsang's burning head, and she must have dozed a little then, for it seemed to her that she and Pemba were in India, starting a new life. When she awoke again, she thought Lobsang looked a little better. She felt comforted, and she lay on the bed beside him. She meant only to rest for a moment, but when Pemba awoke soon afterwards to take a turn at keeping watch, she found Kalsang and Lobsang in a quiet peaceful sleep.

Small Stories – 1

1. In Russia, a farm-worker's little girl was lost. She was only three years old, and the weather was bitterly cold. People from the village looked for her in vain, and when darkness came they still had not found her. Her mother and father did not think she could possibly live through the snowy night.

Early in the morning, however, the little girl came walking down the hill.

"A big dog stayed with me and licked my face," she said. Some of the village people walked back the way the child had come, and there they found a wolf. Marks and footprints in the snow showed that the wolf had kept the little girl warm all night, and must certainly have saved her life.

. . . . . .

2. It is said that, long ago, Saint Francis visited Malaysia. He was walking along a sandy beach when he dropped his rosary. He looked and looked but he could not find it. Then a crab came up to him carrying the rosary on its back. Saint Francis picked up the rosary and made the sign of the cross over the crab. That kind of crab has had the mark of a cross on its back ever since.

3. One of the oldest trees in the world is in Sri Lanka. It is supposed to be more than two thousand two hundred years old, and was grown from a branch brought to the country by a princess in the third century before Christ. The branch was cut from the sacred tree under which the Lord Buddha had sat.

Another ancient tree is a giant oak in America. It is more than seventy-three metres high and is said to be between two thousand and three thousand years old. It is called the Big Tree of Lamar, and it was used as a council tree by a tribe of Red Indians.

. . . .

4. A cello player who was travelling by air, did not want his cello to be put in the luggage compartment of the plane.

"Then you will have to buy a passenger ticket at the full price," he was told, "and the cello can occupy the seat beside you."

So the cello player did so, and when the stewardess brought along free food and drink, he insisted that his cello should receive the same as himself.

Karli and Kit

Karli and Kit were young wild cats. They were not tame cats gone wild. They were real wild cats, of the kind that once roamed freely in the lonely places of Great Britain and Europe and part of Asia. The only place where wild cats still live in Great Britain today is among the mountains of northern Scotland. It was there that the mother wild cat had made a nest in a narrow cleft among the rocks. It was there that Karli and Kit opened their eyes for the first time when they were about ten days old.

At first they were interested only in keeping warm and cosy, and drinking their mother's milk. Then as they grew older they began to wonder what there was beyond the narrow slit of light at the entrance of the den. Sometimes at night or at dawn or dusk their mother would go out, and when she came back, her yellow-grey fur would feel damp and cold, and the brown stripes on her body and tail would look darker because they were wet with dew or rain.

She began to bring back tasty little tit-bits for Karli and Kit. She brought grasshoppers and beetles and sometimes small mice and birds. Soon there came a time when she took her kittens out to learn to hunt for grasshoppers and beetles for themselves. Then early one morning she took them to the river to teach them to catch fish.

There was a sweet, damp smell of heather and grass and rocks. The kittens looked in surprise at the river winding its way through the valley. Kit was still rather sleepy and a little nervous of the strange noise of the water, but Karli was wide awake and eager for adventure. The mother took them to a flat rock with the river washing round it. She showed them how to lean over a little and dip one paw into the flowing water. She showed them how to watch for a fish and then to make a sudden grab at it and pull it out.

"You try, Kit," she said in her own way. Kit tried. She dabbled her paw in the water and clutched at a passing fish. She was not very good at it yet, and after a while she gave up and started eating one of the small fish her mother had caught.

"I'll try," said Karli. He was quite sure that he would catch a fish first time. He crouched at the edge of the rock and watched. He saw a slim black shadow in the water. It was a fish. He was too quick, too sure of himself. He dabbed wildly at it with his paw. He leaned over too far. There was a splash, and he found himself in the water, being carried along downstream.

Wild cats can swim well, but Karli was too frightened and surprised to know what to do.

"Catch hold of that branch!" screamed his mother, hoping he would see the long low hanging branch lying on the water a little further down.

"Stay there!" she said to Kit, and she bounded along the bank, jumping from rock to rock. She knew that if Karli did not struggle too much he would be washed towards the bank at the point where the low branch lay. She was there before him. She leaned over and grabbed the back of his neck in her teeth. She pulled him on to the bank. For a moment he stood there, wet and still very surprised. His first go at fishing had been a failure.

Meanwhile Kit had found herself all alone on the rock. She did not like that at all. She wanted to be near her mother, so she started running along the bank –

over rocks and stones and through rambling plants and tufts of coarse grass.

Suddenly she froze with fear. A great shadow hung above her. She did not know what it was, but she knew she was in danger. At the same moment the mother cat looked that way. She saw Kit crouching in a tuft of grass, and she saw a golden eagle hovering above with outspread wings, with cruel talons poised to strike.

Few creatures are so fierce or so brave as a wild cat. The mother pounced upon Kit, pushing her into a clump of bushes. The eagle's attention was now caught by the mother. His great, dark wings tore through the air as he swooped down towards her. Her next action took him quite by surprise. She stretched up towards him on her strong back legs. She struck out at him with her front paws. Her claws were sharp and cruel. Her fierce hiss was enough to dismay even an eagle.

The eagle's talons touched her and drew blood. She clawed at his face and his neck. It became a silent, deadly struggle. There was no one to watch. There was no one to see how brave the wild cat was – only Karli who gazed from the bank, only Kit who peered from the bushes. Again and again the mother stretched up on her strong back legs and struck at the eagle with her front paws. Flying down and up again, the eagle fought back, but he was young and so surprised at not getting his own way that soon he gave up.

He flew up into the sky and away and away into the distance. Then the mother cat called Karli and Kit and licked them both with her rough tongue. Then she led them back to the safety of their home. One by one the cat family crept through the cleft in the rock – Karli, Kit and the mother. They curled up together in their den and were soon fast asleep.

The Story of Bub

Wars always bring sadness and suffering. The Thirty Years War raged in Germany from 1618 to 1648. It started with German fighting against German, but many other countries of Europe joined in as time passed. It was a particularly cruel war because bands of soldiers plundered the homes of innocent people living in lonely farms and quiet villages. Many of these people had no idea what the fighting was about.

An author who lived through those times wrote a story showing how the war affected the life of a young boy. The author himself was kidnapped by soldiers at the age of ten, and parts of the story are based on his own adventures. It is called "The Adventurous Simplicissimus" and is a huge thick book. It is written in German, but many of the words are strange and not used today.

Here, in English, in a simpler form, is the first part of the story.

. . . . .

His family called him Bub, which was a nickname taken from the German word for "boy". He was a simple, slow-thinking child, but the pace of life itself was slow at that time and he fitted very happily into it.

He lived with his parents and his grown-up sister, on his father's farm. His father kept cattle, sheep, pigs and goats. He grew a few crops and vegetables, and he paid a servant girl and a few workers who lived on the farm.

These were the only people Bub had ever seen – just his own family and the farm workers. He had never been beyond the surrounding woods and fields. He had never seen any house other than his own. This, he thought, was the whole world.

He learned early to take his part in running the farm. At first his father put him in charge of one old sow. Then he had to look after a herd of goats. Then he was given the job of caring for the flock of sheep. This was a great honour. He would wander happily with them on the hillside, keeping his eyes open for wolves and playing merry little tunes on his pipes.

Then, in a single evening, when Bub was ten years old, everything changed. A band of soldiers came riding on horseback over the hill. "The iron men" he called them, probably because of the helmets they wore. They were members of a raggle-taggle army, ill-paid, and often not paid at all. They were loud-voiced, cruel ruffians, whose only food and drink was that which they could steal from farmers and defenceless villagers.

They swarmed into Bub's house as if it were their own. They bound the family and the workers. They tormented them with cruel jokes. They demanded to be told where anything of value might be hidden. They helped themselves to everything eatable that they could lay their hands on. They emptied the feathers from the mattresses, and filled the covers with meat and fruit and bottles of wine, and with cloths and blankets and clothes and pewter dishes and plates. They gathered up tables and chairs and stools and set them on fire at the back of the house.

Bub was busy with his own jobs at the time, and his heart beat fast with fear as he heard thuds and crashes

and shrieks and cries. He did not understand at all what was happening, and no one seemed to notice him. He went into the stable to give water to the horses, which was something he always did during the late afternoon.

"Bub," came a weak voice from the floor. He looked down and saw his mother's servant girl. She was lying bound among the straw, and her voice sounded as if she were ill.

"Bub, run away," she said. "You see how cruel these men are. If they find you, they will tie you up and carry you away with them."

"But where are my mother and father?"

"Somewhere – tied up. Run away Bub. Go now, quickly."

Puzzled, bewildered, frightened, Bub slipped out of the house and across the farmyard into the woods.

"What shall I do?" he thought. "Where shall I go?"

He had never been far into the wood. He did not know the way at all, and the sun was already setting. He crouched down behind a bush. Loud noises echoed through the trees. What was happening in his home? Night came and the sounds were hushed. Then suddenly in the darkness, a nightingale sang. This was a sweet, familiar sound. Bub felt comforted a little, and at last he fell asleep.

He woke early, when the sky was pink with dawn and the morning star was shining. He stood up and brushed himself down.

"I will go home and find my mother and father," he thought. He walked back through the trees, but fear walked with him, for a strange smell hung upon the air, a strong smell of fire and smoke. Then as he came into the open, he saw his father's house, now only a bare framework of blackened, smouldering beams. The soldiers had burned and destroyed it!

He ran towards it. He was filled with horror, but he somehow expected his mother or father, or his sister, to come running up to him. But no one came.

Then he heard a harsh shout.

"Come here boy!"

Bub turned and saw a group of soldiers sitting on the grass. They shouted again, but their talk was strange to him and he did not know what they wanted him to do. He stood still, as if frozen to the spot. One of the men raised a clumsy gun and shot at him. He ran in terror. He stumbled and fell. He landed face downwards, sprawling on the ground. He was too frightened to move. This, perhaps, was a good thing, for the soldiers thought he was dead and after a while they gathered up their booty, and loaded it on to their horses and rode away.

All day long, Bub lay on the ground. Not only were his muscles tight with fear, but he had not the heart to do anything else. His home was a heap of ashes. His mother and father and sister must be dead. The farm workers and the servants must be dead too. There was no one to help or advise him. His whole world had been destroyed.

Only when dusk came did he sit up and look around him, and then stand up and stretch his stiff legs and arms. What should he do? Where should he go? He walked further into the wood, frightened, hungry, thirsty, cold. He found a great hollow tree trunk lying on its side. It offered him a little shelter. He crept into it and slept.

. . . . . .

Each day now became the same as all the other days. He wandered deeper and deeper into the forest. Sometimes he found berries to eat, or little winding streams where he could ease his thirst. At night he slept among bushes, or in fallen, hollow trees. He went on and on, further and further away from home. He had so little idea of how to look after himself in the wild that he thought he would surely die.

Then one evening as he settled down to sleep, he heard a voice lifted up in prayer. Who could it be? He crept forward and peered through the trees. There he saw a tall man with grey hair hanging down over his shoulders. He had a thin, pale face and a tangled beard. He wore a long brown robe with a chain around his waist, and he had a crucifix hanging round his neck. Bub had no time to notice that his expression was a kind one. He was so overcome with fear and terror that he fell forward noisily and fainted at the hermit's feet.

He knew nothing of what happened next, but when he opened his eyes again, he found himself lying on the ground with his head on the hermit's lap. He struggled wildly. He wanted to get up and run away.

"Don't be afraid," said the hermit gently. "God has sent you to me so that I may help you. Let me give you something to eat. I can see that you are starving and weary."

But Bub burst into noisy crying, and the more the hermit tried to comfort him, the more he cried. Then at last he let the hermit lead him to his own small hut, and give him fruit and a little cake of rough bread to eat.

The kind old man asked no questions. He knew that Bub was too tired to talk. He gave him his own bed of branches and leaves on the floor of the hut. He sat beside him and talked softly to him, until Bub fell asleep.

Some time in the middle of the night Bub awoke for a moment and saw the moon shining through the chinks in the roughly-made branch roof. He heard the hoot of an owl in a nearby tree, and he heard the hermit singing softly, a hymn of praise.

So, deep in the forest, far from anywhere, a new life began for Bub. It was a hard, rough life with no comforts, but it was also a good life, because the hermit was a kind man and he took delight in teaching this lonely, simple child. He taught him where to find nuts and wild apples and wild cherries. He showed him which insects and small creatures would provide food. He showed him how to crush wild corn and bake it in little cakes on the ashes of the fire. He showed him how to drink through a hollow reed and how to catch fish from the stream. He told him Bible stories and taught him hymns and sacred songs. He taught him to give thanks to God for everything.

One day Bub saw the hermit holding a book in his hands, and muttering as if he were talking to it. Books were rare in those days, belonging only to scholars and priests and the very rich. Bub had never seen one before, and had no idea what it could be. But it seemed to him that the hermit must be holding a conversation with it.

Later he picked the book up himself and turned the pages. He saw some pictures printed from woodcuts. He saw people and sheep. He spoke to the people and asked them questions, but they did not answer him. He grew impatient.

"You have mouths. Why don't you answer me? You spoke to my father (the hermit). Why don't you speak to me?" Then he noticed that there was a picture of a house on fire.

"Your house is on fire!" he exclaimed excitedly. "Wait, I will put it out for you." Bub stood up, intending to get some water to throw over the picture. The hermit however had been standing behind him, listening to him in amusement.

"No, no," he said. "There's no danger."

"But can't you see?" cried Bub. "The house is burning. The iron men have set fire to it."

"No," replied the hermit. "These people are not alive. The pictures are not real. They have been drawn so that we can see what things looked like in olden times."

"But they must be alive, these people," insisted Bub. "I heard you talking to them a little while ago."

"No, no, dear child," said the hermit, smiling at Bub's simplicity. "These people cannot talk. I know what the pictures are about, by looking at these little black marks on the pages. We call it 'reading'. When you thought I was talking to the pictures, I was really reading."

"Oh!" said Bub. This was quite a new idea to him. "When I am a man," he added, "I should like to learn to look at these little black marks and find out what they say."

"I will teach you now, my son," said the hermit. "I will teach you now, but you will have to be patient and work hard."

The hermit picked up a broken bit of birch bark, and on its smooth side he scratched the letters of the alphabet and taught them to Bub. Then with a stick, he showed him how to write them on the ground.

. . . . .

So Bub learned how to read and write. He loved the hermit, and the hermit looked after him as though he were his own son. He gave him a new name – Simplicissimus – meaning "The Most Simple One", but Bub grew up to be a wise and important man, and he never forgot the hermit's teaching.

Adapted from the German

Chess Stories

Chess is an old, old game. It was mentioned in writing in the late sixth century, but it had been played long, long before that. Some authors believe it started four thousand years ago in one of the ancient civilisations. Some think that King Solomon (of the Bible) played it, and others say that it was invented by Adam himself (the first man created by God). Probably it started in India, and spread quite quickly to many other countries.

It was a war game of princes and kings and noblemen. The chessboard and the chess pieces were made of precious materials – gold or silver, mother-of-pearl or ivory, amber, marble or tortoiseshell, rock crystal, amethyst, brass, pewter or pottery. They were often mentioned in wills and passed down through the same families for generations.

Some Eastern princes had courtyards laid out with black and white stone slabs; and women from their harems took the place of the chessmen. Others built open-air "boards", and used such large and heavy chess pieces that servants had to stand by to move them as required.

Lesser people made their chessmen of cheaper materials – wood or metal, bone or horn, glass or shells. In the desert, Arabs marked boards on the sand and

played with pebbles. In the cold north lands, walrus tusks were used. In Sumatra, people made new pieces for each game. They cut them from fresh palm leaves or bamboos.

The materials used depended mainly on the climate and customs of the different countries. The shapes of the pieces sometimes differed too. One country might use a tower, another an elephant, a ship, a camel, a chariot, a tent or a bear. Quite a lot of history can be learned from sets of chessmen. How did the bishops of the period dress? What sort of soldiers fought in the armies? What sort of armour did they wear? What sort of chairs did the kings and queens use?

Some of the most important old chessmen yet found are known as the Lewis Chessmen. Lewis is a Scottish island in the Outer Hebrides, where in the spring of 1831, a peasant discovered seventy-eight chessmen. They were hidden in a small stone cavity buried four and a half metres down in a sandbank. The sea had beaten against the hiding place for centuries, but only in that particular spring had it exposed the treasure.

Some people think the chessmen may have been English, but the general opinion is that they were made in Iceland in the eleventh or twelfth century. They were carved from walrus tusks, and were probably part of the stock of a travelling pedlar. It is thought that he was bringing them from Iceland to sell in Scotland, when the ship in which he was travelling was wrecked.

Either the bag of chessmen was washed up on the island by the waves, or else the pedlar swam ashore with it. He may have hidden the chessmen himself while he sought food and shelter, but there is also a story that he was attacked and robbed by a local shepherd. The shepherd hid the bag, but for some reason never came back to claim it.

Experts believe that the chessmen remained in the sandbank for seven centuries. They can tell that the pieces were carved in the eleventh or twelfth century by the clothing of the kings and bishops and knights.

These chessmen have full beards, a fashion that went out about 1066. The knights wear plain cone-shaped helmets instead of the more fancy shape of later days. The helmets have a strip coming forward to protect the nose, a type that became common in the twelfth century. The bishops wear mitres. These were not worn before the beginning of the eleventh century.

Sixty-seven of the Lewis chessmen are now in the British Museum for everyone to see. The other eleven are in a museum in Edinburgh, Scotland.

. . . .

One of the world's most skilful chess players was José Capablanca, a Cuban who lived from 1888 to 1943. When he was a small child, less than five years old, he walked into his father's study one day and found him playing chess with a friend. Both men were beginners and neither of them played at all well. José stood quietly beside them and watched them. He had never seen the game before and he was interested in the chess pieces – the king, the queen, the bishop and the knight. He wanted to pick them up and feel the shapes, but he contented himself with simply looking.

The next day the two men played again, and little José watched them as before.

On the third day they played again and once more José stood beside the table, watching. Soon his father made a wrong move. José, small as he was, saw this and expected the other man to mention it. He, however, did not notice. After a while the game finished and José's father had won.

"Your game," said his friend.

"But Father, you cheated!" protested José. "You made a wrong move." The two men looked in amazement at the small child. What did he know about chess!

"If you're going to stay in the room, José," said his father, "you'll have to keep quiet."

"But Father, you cheated. Look, you picked up this one from here and put it there. You're not supposed to do that."

"How do you know anything about chess? How did you learn?"

"I didn't learn, Father, but I know I could beat you."

"That's impossible. You don't even know how to set out the pieces properly." However, the father and the child played, and José won, and that was the beginning of his chess career.

. . . . . .

There are many legends about chess. Here is one of them, in which it is stated that the game was invented by an Indian called Sissa. He presented it to the king, who was very pleased.

"It is a good way to train for war," said the king. "It is also a tribute to religion and a glory to the world. I will reward you. You may ask me for anything you desire."

"Thank you, Your Majesty," replied Sissa. "Then this is my wish. I wish for one grain of wheat to be placed on the first square of the chess board. I wish for two grains of wheat to be placed on the second square, and four grains of wheat on the third square. I wish for the grains to be doubled on each succeeding square until there is wheat on the very last square. It is the wheat on the last square that I wish to receive."

"That is not very much to ask for," said the king, but when he had worked it out, he said, "There is not enough wheat in the whole world to give you. Your cleverness in thinking of this wish is even greater than your cleverness in inventing the game."

The number of grains would be:

9 223 372 036 854 775 808

If they were spread over England they would cover the whole country to a depth of 11·6 metres.

A Page of Riddles

Q. What do you call a burning jacket?
A. A blazer.

Q. What is the difference between a sick cow and an angry crowd?
A. One moos badly and the other boos madly.

Q. Why did the bees go on strike?
A. They wanted shorter working flowers and more honey.

Q. Which hand should you use for stirring tea?
A. Neither. You should use a spoon.

Q. A lorry carrying hairs for a wig factory crashed on the motorway. What did the police do?
A. They combed the area.

Q. Five hundred leadless pencils were stolen from a pencil factory. What did the police say?
A. They said the burglary was pointless.

The Wreck of the *Strathmore*

In April of the year 1875 the sailing ship *Strathmore* was waiting to leave London docks for New Zealand. She was an iron ship built in Dundee, and this was to be her maiden voyage. She was carrying a crew of thirty-eight and a cargo of railway iron and gunpowder. She was also carrying fifty passengers, mainly people who were planning to settle in New Zealand. Most of them wanted to buy land and do farming, but there were others with hopes of striking gold. Most of them of course were men, but there were a few families too, and among them was Mrs Wordsworth and her grown-up son, Charles.

Probably her husband was dead, and she and Charles were wanting to start a new and perhaps more prosperous life in New Zealand. It took a great deal of courage to travel so far in those days. The voyage could be expected to take between three and four months; and living quarters would be crowded and uncomfortable. Meals would usually consist of salt fish and hard ships' biscuits, often crawling with weevils. People took their own boxes of blankets, dishes and cutlery and whatever else they could carry. Captains were sometimes strange, unreliable characters; and fights and disagreements often took place among the crews. Added to that, were the chances of illness and storms and bad weather, and the everlasting tossing of the sea.

Mrs Wordsworth was certainly very brave to start out at all. Charles may have been young enough to regard it all as a great adventure, or old enough to think that it was worth the risks and the hardships. The captain of the *Strathmore* – Captain McDonald – seemed a steady man and the crew were said to be first-class seamen. So Mrs Wordsworth did her best to stifle her fears and to look forward to a sunny future.

The *Strathmore* left London on April the nineteenth. She made her way down the English Channel. The wind filled her sails, and proudly she sped into the Atlantic Ocean on this, her first voyage.

The weeks went by. She sailed past the west coast of Africa. She rounded the Cape of Good Hope and sailed into the Indian Ocean.

"The worst is over," thought the passengers. "It will be a straight run now to Australia, and then to New Zealand."

Two months passed – more than two months. It was the evening of June the thirtieth. A thick fog came down and hid the sea and the sky. Captain McDonald was not worried. He felt fairly sure of his position. He set his course to take him – as he thought – well south of the Crozet Islands. Then he went to bed.

Mrs Wordsworth slept and woke, slept and woke through the night as she usually did. People were breathing heavily all round her, murmuring in their sleep, tossing in their blankets. Then at half past four in the morning she heard a great crash. The ship gave a fearful shudder, and everything that was loose fell to the floor and slid backwards across the boards. The worst had happened. The ship had struck rocks. Her fore-end was held up between them, but her stern sank below water at once and a hole in her plating let the sea in, unchecked.

"Charles!" cried Mrs Wordsworth.

"Up on deck, Mother," he said.

Mrs Wordsworth clutched at a blanket, but it was

jerked from her hand, and she scrambled up on deck in only a nightdress. Many passengers were in a similar state, milling to and fro as if in a nightmare. Some clambered on to the roof of the deck-house, and a few climbed up into the rigging. The voice of the captain was heard shouting,

"Goodbye. It's all over. Save yourselves in the life boats if you can." Next moment he and the first mate, and many of the passengers were swept off the deck and drowned.

Mrs Wordsworth was lucky. She was pushed on to one of the boats in the darkness, with Charles and about sixteen other men. The wave that swept so many people off the deck tossed the lifeboat clear of the wreck. As the men rowed away from the *Strathmore*, the morning light began to reveal their position. The ship was jammed fast on the rocks, some of which rose blackly from the

water to a height of twenty-one metres. A little distance ahead was the dim outline of a small rocky island – one of the Crozet group, known as "The Twelve Apostles". Thankfully some time later Mrs Wordsworth stumbled ashore.

This was July the first. In that part of the world it was mid-winter. It was fairly near the Antarctic Circle, so it was bitterly cold. Mrs Wordsworth was wet through and shivering. A kind sailor took the shirt off his own back and gave it to her, and another gave her an overcoat. During the afternoon the second mate and some of the crew took another boatload to safety, but some people had to spend a second night on the wreck – in the rigging and on the deck-house roof.

At dawn next morning they too were rescued. Some of them were badly frost-bitten and one man died. There were now forty-eight survivors, and they began hopefully to explore their island. Luckily it possessed a spring of fresh water, but apart from that there seemed little to give comfort. The island was a bleak, desolate rock, with no trees or shelter of any kind. Nothing grew there except moss and patches of thin grass, but thousands of seabirds screamed and swooped around.

"We'll save what we can from the ship," said the second mate. "Then in a few days we'll row across to the next island." This appeared to be about nine or ten kilometres distant, and looked more promising.

The first few days ashore were very busy ones. Some people searched the island for firewood. They gathered up a pile of driftwood – enough to keep a fire going for a month perhaps. Some of the crew made risky journeys to the wreck and brought back everything they could find:

    2 barrels of gunpowder
    1 case of jam
    1 case of boots
    Some cases of port, wine, rum, gin and brandy
    8 tins of sweets
    Some tarpaulin and sailcloth

> A few clothes
> A few biscuits
> Some matches in tin boxes
> A passenger's box containing blankets, knives and spoons, and a few other things.

For the first three nights on the island, Mrs Wordsworth and Charles slept in a kind of open cave, with icicles hanging above their heads, and frost settling on their faces. By the fourth night they had a rough lean-to shelter made of turf and stones, with a roof of sailcloth. The biscuits were soon eaten, and the only possible food seemed to be seabirds roasted on the fire. These upset Mrs Wordsworth almost at once and she became ill. She was the only woman survivor, and people were very kind to her. She was given a pair of trousers, some woollen stockings and a few other things to protect her from the cold. She also received a pair of brand new boots. No one else had this good fortune, for the boots in the box all proved to be women's, and much too small for any of the men.

The tide washed a few more things ashore from the *Strathmore*, and the members of the crew still dreamed of voyaging to the next island. One night, however, a violent storm swept the boats out to sea, and the wreck itself sank from sight. Now the castaways were indeed alone and stranded in this desolate place.

The second mate divided the people into six groups. Each group was to prepare its own food – albatross, penguins, other seabirds and moss day after day. The moss had long, trailing roots, and the people were so hungry that they often ate dirt and all. Everyone was given a few sips of wine or spirits every night as long as they lasted. Mrs Wordsworth and Charles were given a rough shelter to themselves at some distance from the other people. Charles did his best to look after his mother, who became so weak and thin that she looked like a skeleton. She could not even turn over at night without his help.

He fried birds' brains for her, and he minced up birds' hearts and livers with moss, mixed with gunpowder and seawater. The nights were bitterly cold and very long, with fifteen hours of darkness. Sleep was always fitful and light, for the ground was usually wet and clothes were always damp. Dreams were nearly always of delicious things to eat, followed by a hungry awakening.

The one good thing was the fire, but soon the driftwood was all burned. The people tried turf as fuel but it was almost useless. Then, by chance, one day someone threw a bird-skin on the fire and it burned with a welcome, oily blaze. There were always plenty of seabird skins, so once again the fire was kept burning.

Water had been carried at first in an old sea boot, but now could be carried in the sweet tins and jars. One tin was also used as a lamp, fed with fat from the birds' skins.

From the very beginning a distress signal was set up on the highest point of the island. It was made from a blanket strung to a mast and hoisted on a tower of stones and turf. Soon, surely, a ship would pass and see it. Soon, surely, rescue would come. The men took it in turns to watch by the signal. If they saw a ship they were to light the beacon fire that was always ready. So week in, week out, they watched and waited and hoped.

Four times they sighted ships. One was as near as five kilometres from The Twelve Apostles rocks. Four times they lit the beacon fires and let the oily bird-skins blaze a signal of distress. Four times they saw a ship pass by, giving no help, giving no sign. On two of the ships, there were people who actually saw the fire and the billowing blanket, and reported it to the ship's officers. The officers said perhaps whalers had made a fire. "It couldn't be a distress signal," they said.

Weeks went by. Months went by. A young boy died. His parents had been drowned on the night of the wreck. Others grew weaker, or fell ill from cold and hunger. Three more men died. By December there were only forty-four survivors.

The year ended. December turned to January; 1875 turned to 1876. Everyone had grown weaker. It was amazing that after six whole months of suffering, they should still be alive. Some said they had given up all hope of ever being rescued, but most of them went on wishing, and longing and waiting.

Then came January the twenty-first. It was evening time and the watchers on the signal hill were preparing to return to the shelter for the night. Then someone saw a ship. At once the fire was lit. The oily bird-skins flamed and flared. The fire blazed and blinked across the southern ocean. There were minutes of terrible fear and uncertainty. Then the watchers saw the ship change course and sail towards the Twelve Apostles.

The men on watch could hardly believe it, and one of them ran in excitement to tell the other people. Those who were strong enough climbed up to the signal post to watch. There was still a time of suspense as the ship anchored off shore. There was still the chance that the crew had not really seen the beacon fire. Then the castaways saw two boats lowered, and rowing towards them. Rescue was coming! No words could describe the joy and excitement, the relief and thankfulness.

The ship was an American whaler called *Young Phoenix*. It was getting dark, so the captain could not rescue all the castaways that night. However he landed some bread and pork on the island, and he took off Mrs Wordsworth and Charles and a few of the weaker men. By a happy chance the captain's wife was with him, and she at once took care of Mrs Wordsworth. She gave her a hot bath, and some clean clothes, and hot food and drink. It was nearly seven months since Mrs Wordsworth had had such luxuries. It was nearly seven months since she had seen another woman. The captain's wife was kindness itself, and as soon as she had made Mrs Wordsworth comfortable, she busied herself looking after the men.

The next morning, as soon as dawn broke, the boats went back to the island and took off the rest of the castaways. Then the *Young Phoenix* set sail towards Africa.

Mrs Wordsworth and Charles looked back at the Crozet Islands. They gazed for the last time at the Twelve Apostles Rocks, rising blackly from the cold, grey sea. They thought of the ship *Strathmore* lying broken and wrecked below, and they murmured a prayer of thankfulness because, in spite of everything, they were still alive.

. . . . . .

The *Young Phoenix* was too small to take all the extra passengers very far, so a few days later she transferred twenty of them to another ship. The others, including Mrs Wordsworth, were landed at Mauritius and taken later to England, where they arrived in March. Only then did people at home hear of the fate of the *Strathmore*.

You would think that after all her sufferings, Mrs Wordsworth would settle quietly in England. She did so, for a few years. Then, with great courage, she and Charles packed their boxes and set off once again for New Zealand. This time they arrived safely; and records show that they bought a piece of land there in 1882. Charles brought up a family of his own – four daughters and a son, and it is possible that some of their descendants are there to this day.

Hiawatha

Hiawatha was a Red Indian chief who lived during the fifteenth century and united several different tribes in peace. Many stories grew up about him, so that today it is quite difficult to separate truth from legend.

He was said to have possessed magic powers, and he taught his people navigation and medicine and arts. He gave them maize for food, and taught them how to grow it and use it.

The American poet, Henry Longfellow, wrote a poem about him in the year 1855. It contains about five thousand lines and is written in a pleasant, musical rhythm. There are many Indian names in it – names for animals, trees and people.

Here are some lines from the section that is called "Hiawatha's Childhood". Hiawatha had been asking his grandmother, old Nokomis, about the stars and the fireflies, about the moon and the rainbow.

When he heard the owls at midnight,
Hooting, laughing in the forest,
"What is that?" he cried in terror;
"What is that," he said, "Nokomis?"
And the good Nokomis answered:
"That is but the owl and owlet,
Talking in their native language,
Talking, scolding at each other."

   Then the little Hiawatha
Learned of every bird its language,
Learned their names and all their secrets,
How they built their nests in Summer,
Where they hid themselves in Winter,
Talked with them whene'er he met them,
Called them "Hiawatha's Chickens".

   Of all the beasts he learned the language,
Learned their names and all their secrets,
How the beavers built their lodges,
Where the squirrels hid their acorns,
How the reindeer ran so swiftly,
Why the rabbit was so timid,
Talked with them whene'er he met them,
Called them "Hiawatha's Brothers".

Henry Wadsworth Longfellow 1807–1882

The Camp

The camp was in India, a level stretch of land in the mountains. It was a special camp for children who had come on the long journey from Tibet, and who were now shabby and hungry and homeless. They had come with their families and friends. They had come to escape from the fighting in Lhasa. They had come to be near their god-king, the Dalai Lama.

The families had not thought too much about what they would do when they actually reached India. Many of the Indians were poor themselves, and though they showed great kindness to the refugees, there was little work they could offer them other than road building. This was the work that Kalsang and Pemba, the two mothers, were doing now. Sadly they had left Dolkar and Diki in the children's camp because they knew that there they would be fed and looked after.

"You must think how lucky you are," Kalsang had said. "Many families came over the mountains as we did, and hundreds and hundreds of children died of cold and hunger. You are lucky to be alive." She had pointed to the gleaming, snow-covered peaks of the Himalayas in the distance, and added,

"Look children. You can see Tibet from here. Look

at it sometimes and think to yourselves that better times will come soon."

. . . .

Four days had passed.

"You are lucky to be alive," Kalsang had said. Lucky to be alive! There were times when Dolkar wished that she were dead. She had borne all the hardships bravely, because Mother had always been beside her, and little brother Lobsang had needed comfort and help; and there had been Pemba and Diki too. Now it was different. She was alone, all alone, and she could not bear it.

She wondered again about Diki.

"Dolkar, look after Diki for me," Pemba had said.

"Yes, of course I will," she had replied. Then almost at once, a brisk, busy lady had swept Diki from her side and wafted her away somewhere else. For four days now, Dolkar had moved among the milling crowds of children and pushed her way into silent, shabby groups, and peered into worried little faces, looking for Diki.

For four days she had asked every nurse or helper she had seen,

"Please where is my little cousin, Diki?"

Some had not understood her language. Some had understood and had said,

"Don't worry dear. She's around somewhere, I expect."

They were so busy. They had so many children to care for. They had so much pity in their hearts, but they had no time at all for one little girl out of hundreds.

Dolkar was not looking for Diki now. She was hiding. She was hiding because all the girls were having their hair cut – not just cut, but shaved close to their heads.

They stood in a line, miserably, dumbly, and watched their long, thick, black tresses fall in a growing heap on the ground. They were passive and obedient. Then, when the cutting and the shaving were finished, each girl in turn clapped her hands to her head as if to protect it from winds that might blow.

"I won't let them cut my hair," said Dolkar to herself. "I won't." She knew that there was a good reason for the operation. Lots of the children had lice. The horrid creatures clung to their hair and sucked at their blood. They spread from child to child and laid their numerous eggs, to hatch and spread a hundredfold.

"I won't let anyone cut my hair," she thought, and she crouched at the back of a tumbledown one-storey wooden building, peeping out from time to time to see when it would be safe to emerge. Suddenly one of the helpers looked up and started walking that way. Afraid of being noticed, Dolkar disappeared round the corner, darted behind a sheltering bush, and then into a group of trees. No one would see her now. A heady breath of freedom filled her lungs and she began to walk downhill. There, some distance below, she saw another large tent and two or three smaller ones and another wooden building. She also saw children playing there. Perhaps it was another part of the camp. Perhaps that was where Diki had been taken. A little surge of hope came to her and she began to run.

Soon she was mingling with the crowds of children below. They were all Tibetan like herself, and on the whole they were a little younger than the children in her own part of the camp. Some were kicking a stone about with a lot of noise and shouting. Some were playing and laughing as if they had not a care in the world. Others were standing about, sad and disconsolate, and others again were lining up for medicine or treatment from an English nurse. Anxiously Dolkar looked from child to child, from face to face, but she could not find Diki.

She looked in one of the tents. It was deserted. She looked in another. It too, was deserted. But no! As she was about to leave it, she saw a movement in the far corner. There was a child lying on a mat on the ground. The child's back was towards Dolkar. It was not Diki. It was nothing like her. Yet something made Dolkar go

forward and take a closer look. The child's head had been shaved and it had been daubed with a mauve lotion. The child was obviously very ill, and with a sinking heart, Dolkar realised that it was indeed Diki. How could she have changed so much in four days? How could the gay, lively little Diki have come to this? Not only was she very ill, but she was also suffering from a skin disease that marked her with big sore patches on her face and her hands.

"Diki, Diki!" whispered Dolkar, but Diki's eyes were glazed and she gave no sign of recognition.

Just then a little girl crept out from the shadows. She waved a hand at Diki and said,

"Do you know her?"

"Yes. She's my cousin. I've been looking for her."

"I'm her friend. My name is Noola," said the little girl. "She's ill. I'm looking after her."

"She's very ill," said Dolkar. "Stay here with her. I'll see if I can get help."

She hurried out to the place where the children were lining up for medical attention. There was an English doctor there now, in a white coat. She went up to him and touched his arm.

"Wait your turn dear," he said brightly. He spoke English and Dolkar did not understand. Fear for Diki made her bold. She tugged at the doctor's arm and tried to pull him away. He tried to shake her off with a puzzled smile. Then he read the desperation in her eyes, and he let Dolkar lead him to the tent where Diki lay. Dolkar never found out what was wrong with Diki but the doctor could tell that it was the result of insufficient food, and weeks of hardship and exposure to the weather. He wrapped a blanket round her and carried her at once to the medical tent, with Dolkar and the little girl following. There was a Tibetan helper there, who spoke both languages.

"We'll keep her in bed here for a few days," she said. "The doctor will look after her."

"My little brother was ill too," explained Dolkar. "We had to take him to a monastery and ask a priest to say prayers for him. We ought to take Diki to a priest."

"What does she say?" asked the doctor.

"She wants to take the little girl to a monastery and ask a priest to say prayers for her."

"Tell her," said the doctor gently, "tell her I will say a little prayer instead."

Dolkar and the little girl hung around outside the medical tent for the rest of the day. Once or twice a nurse took pity on them and tried to tell them in sign language that the doctor would make Diki better.

"Don't worry," she said. "Don't worry."

Once a Tibetan helper passed by. She stopped, and stepped back and stared in surprise at Dolkar's long, black hair.

"Now how, *how* did you get left out?" she demanded. Then Dolkar realised that here too, all the children had had their hair shaved.

"I'll do it this minute, before you disappear again," said the helper, and this time Dolkar submitted meekly and obediently. Now that she had found Diki, she did not mind quite so much about losing her hair. Besides, if she looked like everyone else, it would be easier for her to stay in this part of the camp unnoticed.

That evening she lined up with the others for a meal. She was probably older than most of the children, but she did not really look any taller. She would stay here all the time and look after Diki. The meal consisted of thin soup and mo-mo. Mo-mo had been her favourite meal at home. It was like little cushions of dough with meat inside. This was different. It was just little cushions of dough full of emptiness, and after the meal everyone was still hungry.

When she went to the medical tent and asked if she could see Diki, the nurse did not recognise her. Dolkar had already learned one word of English that day.

"Please," she said. "Please." The nurse guessed then that she wanted to visit someone, and she said,

"I'm sorry, you can't. Oh, all right. One quick look through the door." So Dolkar peeped round the tent door and saw that Diki was asleep. Then she crept quietly away again.

There was no difficulty about finding somewhere to spend the night. She simply took Diki's place on the mat in the tent where she had first found her. The little girl Noola, Diki's friend, lay beside her, and eight other children had to share one big blanket with them. The tent was full of children lying in rows – one touching the next. Dolkar kept her chuba on. (The chuba is the cross-over garment that most Tibetans wear.) She had not taken it off since she had left home. How long ago was that?

She saw some children sitting up, saying prayers,

and that reminded her of her own. She took out her prayer beads and moved them slowly along the string and muttered her prayers. Most of the children fell asleep as soon as their heads touched the mats. Dolkar finished her prayer and lay down. Diki's little friend snuggled up beside her, like a sleepy kitten. She was just like everyone else – small and lonely and wanting her mother. Dolkar put her arms round her, and felt suddenly very old.

Noola was already asleep, but Dolkar lay for a long time with her eyes wide open. She felt a little happier now. She had found Diki. Diki was ill, but she was being looked after in the hospital tent. The doctor and the nurses were kind. They would make her better, just as the abbot-doctor had made little brother Lobsang better at the monastery.

"Better times will come soon," Mother had said. Dolkar closed her eyes and repeated it to herself. Courage and hope came creeping back to her, and she fell asleep.

Sleeping Heroes

Many countries have stories about some hero or king or leader who lies sleeping in a cave or a secret place in the mountains, and who will awake one day and return to help his people.

Britain

King Arthur was a military hero of the sixth century. Stories about him have always been a mixture of truth and legend, and there are many parts of the country that claim to be his resting place. It is said that he and his queen and all his knights are sleeping together in a large cave in Northumberland near the great Roman wall. With them are sixty pairs of dogs, and lying near the king is a royal garter and a horn, and a sword of stone. If someone could find the cave and blow the horn and cut the garter with the sword, the whole company would awaken.

Legend says that one day a shepherd did find the cave. He pushed his way to the entrance, through a maze of bushes and brambles, and he found himself in an underground room where a fire was burning mysteriously without fuel. He saw the noble company lying on couches; and he saw the horn, the garter, and the stone sword on a table near the king. He picked up the sword, and all the people moved and murmured in their sleep. He cut the garter and everyone sat up with open eyes, but he forgot to blow the horn. So, as he put the sword back on the table, King Arthur and his queen and all his knights and dogs fell back again into a deep sleep. There they sleep still.

Ireland
The Irish have a hero who lives under a lake in the Land of Perpetual Youth. It is said that he rides forth on a white horse each May morning to see how Ireland is faring. No one ever sees him, but everyone knows that he is waiting for the right moment, when he will lead his people to victory.

Germany
Frederick the First was one of the early kings of Germany, as well as Emperor of the Holy Roman Empire. He had long yellow hair and a reddish beard, and he became known by the name of Barbarossa or Red Beard. He was wise and strong, and he helped to bring order to Germany.

It is said that he is waiting in a cavern in a mountain in Germany. He sits at a stone table with the knights and dwarfs of his court around him. He has also some ravens which act as messengers. They fly in and out of the cavern, bringing him news of the outside world. If Germany needs Barbarossa he will rise up and lead his country to victory and peace.

Yugoslavia

King Mathias also has ravens to keep watch over the mountain cave where he now sleeps, after conquering the Turks long ago. It is said that a lime tree will grow on the mountain one Christmas night. It will bloom at midnight and then die. A few months later, on St George's Day, King Mathias will awake and come out of the cave. He will hang his shield on the tree and it will burst into bloom again to give promise of a brighter future for his people.

Canada

Glooskap was supposed to be a sort of god-chief of some of the Indian tribes in what is now Canada. He was able to work magic, and he set the land free from monsters and giants. The Indians say that he sailed away at last in his canoe until he came to his father's hunting grounds. There he lives in a great tent making arrows year after year. When his tent is quite full of arrows, Glooskap will come back to fight his last battle and to bring peace and happiness to his people.

Denmark

Holger the Dane is the hero of many stories and songs. He sleeps in a mountain cave, and his beard has become so long that it has grown right through the table in front of him. He will awake one day when Denmark needs him.

. . . .

Sometimes these stories are part of a strong belief, but often they are just a longing and a hope for the world to become a better place.

Little Boy Lost

The little boy was lost in France when he was about two and a half years old. His name was John. His father, Hilary Wainwright, was an Englishman, and his mother, Lisa, was Polish. They had married in Paris, and it was there that John had been born. It was the time of the Second World War, and like many other couples, Hilary and Lisa had only a few snatched hours of happiness together from time to time, and long separations in between. So Hilary had seen his son only once, on the day after his birth.

The baby had been tucked up in his cot, at the foot of Lisa's bed in the French flat. Hilary had gazed at the little red, crumpled face and the dark hair. He had noticed a small pink velvet dog propped up beside the baby. The dog was Binkie, and it had always stood on the mantelpiece until then. It had bright beady eyes, and one velvet ear sticking up and one flopping down.

Hilary had won it at a fair and given it to Lisa. They had been very happy then. They had thought that the war would soon be over and that they would be able to go to England and make their home there.

But it had not worked out that way. The war had gone on from year to year, spreading suffering and tragedy. Hilary, on secret service in England, had received a notice from the Foreign Office saying that Lisa had been killed in France. He had made many enquiries about the baby, but had heard not a word about him. He guessed that one of Lisa's friends would take care of the child, and he longed for the day when the war would end and he could go to Paris and bring him home to England.

. . . . . .

It was 1945. The war had ended at last, and Hilary was sitting in the small bare waiting room of a Catholic orphanage in a town eighty kilometres outside Paris. Pierre, a friend of his, had worked for many months trying to trace the little lost boy for him. He had followed up the short life stories of several children, and then found that, for one reason or another, they could not belong to Hilary.

"But this one," he had written, "this one might be yours." Pierre had explained to the Mother Superior, and had arranged for Hilary to visit the orphanage to see the little boy. The nuns were used to having people come these days to claim their children. Some of the parents had been prisoners of war. Families had been broken up and separated. The little boy was not told, of course, that Hilary might be his father. He was told only that an Englishman was coming to take him out for a walk.

The little boy at the orphanage was called Jean, which is French for John. No one had known his real name, for he had called himself Bou-bou when he had arrived. It was just chance that the nuns had chosen the name of Jean for him.

"Still," thought Hilary. "It makes things seem hopeful somehow."

He waited. He had no idea what the child would look like. He himself had dark hair, but Lisa had been very fair.

"What will he look like?" he thought. "How shall I be able to tell if he is my child or not? Shall I know at once, by instinct, one way or the other?"

It was half past five. He waited, cold and nervous and full of troubled thoughts. Then the door handle rattled, and a little five-year-old boy came in. This must be, it *must* be Hilary's son.

Hilary looked at the little boy, and his heart sank.

He was a thin, frail-looking child in a black overall, with sleeves that were too short. He had long thin legs and he wore thick, coarse socks and shabby black boots that looked much too big for him. He had a pale little face, black hair, and huge dark, wistful eyes. This surely could not be John. He looked like a foreign child.

"He can't be mine," thought Hilary. He could speak fluent French and he knew he ought to greet the child and clasp his hand. Yet he just stood there, staring and saying nothing.

Then the Mother Superior came in with a small black coat on her arm.

"Jean," she said. "This is Monsieur Wainwright, the Englishman I told you about. He's going to take you out for a walk. He will be staying in the town for a few days, so perhaps he will take you out again tomorrow and the next day."

"If you take Jean out every day for a week or more," she had said to Hilary beforehand, "then I'm sure you will be able to tell whether he is your son or not."

She put the coat on the little boy and buttoned it up tightly.

"You'll be back by half past seven, won't you?" she said.

Now they were outside the gate, Hilary tall and uncertain, and the little boy, excited and shy. The town was a very uninteresting one, shabby and poor. A cold grey mist hung upon the air.

"Whatever shall we do for two hours?" thought Hilary.

"Is there anywhere special you'd like to go?" he asked. Jean's face lit up, and he said eagerly,

"Oh, monsieur, I should like to see the trains. There is a level crossing. I have never been there, but I know it is this way – down the hill. Robert told me."

Jean walked eagerly beside Hilary, but sometimes in his excitement he would run a few steps ahead and then come back again, and look up at Hilary and smile.

"There's the level crossing," said Hilary as they reached the bottom of the hill. They were lucky, for just at that moment the tall posts came dropping down, lowering the swinging iron rods that sealed off the road like a curtain.

Jean caught hold of Hilary's coat, and watched in wonder. There was a chug and a chuff, and a goods train came rattling up the line. Its wagons were filled with coal and they passed one after another, one after another, until the very last had rumbled out of sight into the distance, and its noise had died away.

"Oh!" murmured the little boy. "I've never seen a train before!"

Never seen a train before! Yet he lived so close to them! Hilary could hardly believe it. He felt hurt and sad to think of all the ordinary everyday things in life that this little boy was missing.

The barrier was still down.

"Perhaps there's another train coming, Jean," he said. Jean waited eagerly. Then it came. It was just an old steam engine this time, puffing noisily by.

"Oh monsieur," shrieked Jean in delight, "it's going backwards!" Hopefully he waited for more, but now the posts went up, and the iron rods swung back into place.

Hilary was cold. There was a café across the road.

"Let's go inside," he suggested. "It will be warmer in there, and we may see some more trains from the window." He led the little boy to an empty table.

"What will you have?" he asked. Then he realised that Jean knew no more about cafés than he did about trains. So he ordered a raspberry drink for him, and watched in sad amusement as the child looked at it in wonder, and gulped it quickly and noisily down.

The time passed very slowly for Hilary. There were many things he was longing to know, longing to ask. But what memories could a little boy be expected to have when he had spent his last few years in an orphanage? Hilary tried to talk of ordinary things, but even this was difficult. He knew from his earlier conversation with the Mother Superior that there were no toys in the orphanage. There was never enough food for the children. They were all thin and undernourished, and many of them were ill. He started telling Jean about the London Zoo – the lions, the tigers, the elephants. He wanted to say, "I'll take you there one day," but he was afraid to say it. How could he tell whether this were his son? How could he promise to take him anywhere?

Soon it was quarter past seven. Hilary was filled with relief.

"We'll have to be going back," he said. The little boy stood up and stared at him with his huge, dark wistful eyes.

"I'll take you out again tomorrow," promised Hilary.

"And the next day?"

"Yes, and the next day."

"Will you take me the day after that?"

"I don't quite know," answered Hilary. How could he tell?

They walked up the hill together and rang the bell at the orphanage. A nun opened the door and smiled kindly at Jean.

"Say 'thank you' to monsieur," she said.

"Thank you, monsieur," said Jean.

. . . . . .

Hilary was staying in a very shabby poor-looking hotel, but it was costing him a great deal in French francs. The days passed slowly, and he spent most of his time sitting in his room reading, and waiting for the evening to come. He was allowed to take Jean out every day at half past five and bring him back at half past seven. The nun who answered the door to him had said that he could walk in without ringing.

"I will see that Jean is always ready for you," she said. "He will be sitting in the hall here every day." Every day! How long was it going to take Hilary to decide whether Jean were his child or not?

On the second day, the little boy's eyes shone as Hilary arrived.

"Where shall we go today?" asked Hilary.

"Please, monsieur, the trains!" This time he chattered eagerly as they walked down the hill together.

"Do you think we shall see the goods train again, monsieur? Does it come from Paris? Robert said he had seen a passenger train once. Do you think we might see a passenger train, monsieur?"

So once again they watched the trains, and then they sat in the café, and Jean gulped a raspberry drink as before. Hilary tried hard to think of something to say – something that might help him to decide.

"When is your birthday, Jean?" he asked.

"I don't have a birthday, monsieur." He paused, then added, "Do you think that is why I never get any presents, monsieur?"

"Oh no," protested Hilary. "It's because of the war. Everyone is too poor to buy presents these days."

"But some of the other boys have presents. A lot of boys have birthdays."

"Jean," put in Hilary, changing the subject abruptly, "my name is Hilary. Have you ever heard that name before?"

"No, monsieur."

"Have you heard the name Lisa – a girl's name?"

"No, monsieur."

"It's no good," thought Hilary. "I can't keep asking him questions. I don't even know what to ask." But at that moment, Jean put a question of his own.

"Did you know Armand?"

"No. Who is he?"

"He was at the orphanage. One day his father came back from the war, and took Armand back home with him." Jean looked steadily at Hilary and went on,

"Luc's father came back too, and took Luc away with him." Then his lips trembled and he added fiercely,

"Why don't my mother and father come and fetch me?"

Slowly the week dragged by. It was very dull in the hotel and Hilary had no one to talk to except one young woman called Nelly, who was on holiday there. She lived in Paris and she tried to persuade him to go back with her.

"I'm going home on Monday evening," she said. "Come with me and I'll show you the sights."

It was tempting. He needed some fun for a change. He began to wonder whether he should stay here and take Jean out again for a few more days, or whether he should go to Paris and have a good time with Nelly. His thoughts were in a turmoil. Day after day he argued with himself – about Nelly and about the little boy.

"If I knew that Jean were my son, I would take him. But I don't know. I have no proof at all. This little boy needs love and a home. I could take him whether he is mine or not. I could comfort him and give him happiness and good food. But I didn't come to France to adopt a child. I came to find John. If I took this boy, my own son might still turn up later –"

He had spoken several times about it with the Mother Superior.

"I have prayed for guidance, monsieur," she had said. "I feel it is right that you should take Jean, even if you are unsure about him. Your instinct has not helped you at all. If you are uncertain about this child, you will probably be just as uncertain about any child. Jean needs a good home. I hoped you might have grown fond of him."

"I have," he had protested, "but I should not want to take the wrong child."

"Shall I take him, or shall I not?" he asked himself a hundred times. "If only I had some proof! If only there were a sign!"

By the end of the week he had made up his mind. He would go to Paris with Nelly on Monday. He would stay a few days with her and then return to London. He would go without the boy. There was nothing to show that he was his own. He worked it out in his mind as he walked away from the orphanage on Sunday evening. He would write a letter to the Mother Superior in the morning and leave it at the orphanage. He would leave tomorrow – Monday evening.

Meanwhile, as he walked back towards the shabby

hotel, his attention was taken by a small crowd of people in the town square. A shooting-booth had been set up, and people were laughing and talking and shooting for prizes. The prizes were standing on some shelves at the back. Hilary glanced at the cheap assortment of toys and ornaments. Then he gasped! There among the prizes stood a small pink velvet dog. It had bright beady eyes. It had one ear sticking up and one ear flopping down.

"Binkie!" thought Hilary. "It's just like Binkie." Memories came flooding into his mind.

"I must win it," he thought and he paid his money and began to shoot. He won the foolish little dog without much effort, and took it back to his room. Then he sat on the edge of the bed and began to write a letter to the Mother Superior. He thanked her for her kindness, and said that he was returning to England, because he had not been able to decide about Jean.

"Meanwhile will you please give him this present," he added.

He wrapped the pink velvet dog in a piece of newspaper and tied it up with string. He sealed up the letter.

"If I change my mind, I can always come back again," he thought. But he knew that if he once took the train to England, he would never return to the orphanage.

There was a train to Paris at half past five on Monday evening. It was the one Nelly was catching. Hilary had agreed to meet her at the station, so that they would travel together. He walked along the grey streets, carrying his small case.

"How thankful I shall be to get out of this place," he said to himself. He thought of course of little Jean. He would be disappointed at missing his walk this evening. He would know by now, for Hilary had sent the letter and the present to the orphanage with one of the maids from the hotel. Jean would know by now. He would be disappointed. He would be hurt.

Hilary tried to push the child from his mind, but he could not. Perhaps he would never be able to do so. He walked on, more slowly now. Soon the grey roof of the station was visible. Hilary stood still, and doubts troubled him again. Should he go into the station and meet Nelly as planned? Should he go to Paris and have a good time with her? What ought he to do? He hesitated a moment. Then he swung round suddenly and walked back towards the orphanage.

The letter and the present were still waiting for the Mother Superior, for she had not been in her office when they had arrived. So the little boy was sitting in the hall expecting Hilary as usual. He was buttoned up in his plain black coat. He was ready.

"Monsieur is a bit late today," said one of the nuns as she passed him. The little boy looked anxious. He went on waiting.

Then the Mother Superior came and sat beside him on the hard bench. She put the newspaper parcel into his hands and said,

"Here is a present for you, Jean."

Eagerly the little boy tugged at the string. His hands were cold and it took him quite a time to unwrap the parcel.

Just as he pulled the last of the paper away, the front door opened and Hilary came in unnoticed. He was just in time to see the look of delight on the little boy's face, and to hear his shout of surprise and joy.

"It's Binkie! It's Binkie come back to me!"

Adapted from the book "Little Boy Lost" by Marghanita Laski, published by The Cresset Press.

Silly Stories

Jan: I can't afford to buy oats any more. It's too expensive. I'm going to train my horse to live without food.

A week later

Carl: Well? How's your horse?

Jan: Just as I had trained it to live without food, it died.

The telephone rang in the middle of the night.
Sleepily, Mike crawled downstairs to answer it.

Voice: Is that one, one, one, one?

Mike: No. It's eleven, eleven.

Voice: Are you sure it's not one, one, one, one?

Mike: Quite sure. It's eleven, eleven.

Voice: I must have the wrong number then. I'm sorry I disturbed you in the middle of the night.

Mike: Oh, that's all right. I had to get up anyway to answer the telephone.

Evonne

Evonne Goolagong was an Australian girl. She belonged to the Aborigine people. The Aborigines had lived in Australia long, long before white men had settled there. They were brown-skinned, gentle people who had learned to understand the hot, desert land. Other races might have died out with hunger and thirst, but the Aborigines were clever enough to find food in the most unlikely places.

They would find tiny plants and insects and small desert mammals to eat. They would hunt kangaroos and wallabies with their spear-sticks and boomerangs. Most of the Aborigines wandered through bush and desert. They walked long, long distances in the burning sun. They moved with the weather. They followed the food supply.

Evonne's father, however, had settled at the small town of Barellan in New South Wales. The country around was flat, with a view of hills in the distance. Farmers kept sheep and grew wheat there, and Evonne's father had become a sheep shearer. There was often work for him near Barellan, and, with the farmers' electric clippers, he could shear two hundred sheep a day.

The family lived in an old tin shack. It was a jolly family of five boys and girls at that time, with three other baby brothers and sisters to follow later. The Goolagongs were the only dark-skinned children in the town, but they did not feel any different from anyone else, and all the children played happily together.

Now the Australians are very keen on outdoor sports, and they are especially keen on tennis. Nearly every small town in the bush has one or two tennis courts, probably made of flattened anthills. Nearly every small town has a tennis club where the children grow up learning to play tennis as soon as they are big enough to hold a racket. There are contests and tournaments between the children of different places, and they will often travel long distances by car to take part.

While Evonne was still a baby, a man called Mr Kurtzman came to live at Barellan, and was kind enough to give some money towards a tennis club for the town. So builders began to put up a red brick building next to the Goolagong home.

"What is it? What is it?" asked some of the children.

"It's a club house," was the answer. "A tennis club for the town. It's going to cost four dollars a year to join."

Evonne's family would not have been able to afford even one dollar, but when the building was finished and the courts were laid out at the side, some kind person paid for the two elder children to join. So Barbara and Larry joined the club, and little sister Evonne watched them play. Soon she herself was old enough to join, and she took great delight in rushing about the courts, hitting the ball with a borrowed racket.

The children took turns in playing on the courts

through the long hot holidays, and some of them became so keen that they would also play early on frosty winter mornings before school, as well as in the evenings when the courts were floodlit. They did not play too seriously, or even very well. They just had fun.

. . . . . .

Far from the dusty little town of Barellan was the city of Sydney with its busy streets and towering skyscrapers and its great bridge across the harbour. In Sydney, a man called Mr Edwards kept a tennis school. He was one of the best tennis coaches in Australia, and he had a good staff and a large number of pupils. Adults and children went to the tennis school. They were taught in classes at first, without using a ball at all. They were taught how to stand, how to move, how to swing their rackets. They had to practise the same movements, the same strokes, over and over again.

During the long Christmas holidays (summer in Australia), Mr Edwards would send some of his teachers into five or six different centres to hold a week's tennis school. This gave country children the chance to learn tennis properly. They would have lessons six days running, and they would learn as much in a week as perhaps the Sydney children might have spread over half a term.

Mr Kurtzman in Barellan thought it would be a good idea to have a week's tennis school there, and Mr Edwards agreed to send two teachers. Most of the children could afford to pay, but no one was left out if he or she could not. So, when Mr Edwards's teachers arrived at Barellan that summer, they found three Goolagongs waiting to be taught. There were Barbara and Larry, and there was Evonne, now eight years old.

The teachers, Mrs Martin and Mr Swan, noticed the Goolagong children almost at once. First they noticed them because they were the only dark-skinned children in the club. Then they noticed them because their tennis clothes were always whiter than those of anyone else, even though their home was the poorest in the

town. Then they noticed them because they moved and played so well. The children were taught in classes much of the time, without using a ball at all. They were taught how to stand, how to move, how to swing their rackets. They had to practise the same movements, the same strokes, over and over again. All three Goolagong children were good, but little Evonne was especially so.

"I'd like Mr Edwards to see her," said Mrs Martin to Mr Swan.

"Yes. So should I. I wonder if she'll be here again next summer when we come."

"Probably not. She's an Aborigine. Some Aborigines are always on the move aren't they?"

"Yes. A pity. She'd make a good player, with some proper training."

The week ended. Mrs Martin and Mr Swan said "Goodbye till next year" and went away. The children took their turns on the tennis courts again and tried to remember what they had been taught. Evonne, in particular, practised and practised and practised.

A year passed. The Christmas holidays came round again, hot and dry and sunny. Mrs Martin and Mr Swan arrived to take the week's tennis school at Barellan. They taught the children in classes of fifteen. They taught them how to stand, how to move, how to swing their rackets. They made them practise the same movements, the same strokes, over and over again. They gave them turns at real games on the courts.

The same children were there from the year before, with a few more who had become old enough to join meanwhile. The same children were there, and with them was Evonne, now nine years old. She had practised all the year. She had not grown much, but she was a little stronger, a little faster, and a lot better at tennis.

Mrs Martin was delighted to see her. She knew there was something special about Evonne, and she felt very strongly that someone ought to help her to get proper training. She could become a tennis star, a champion!

"She's wonderful," said Mrs Martin to Mr Swan. "We *must* ask Mr Edwards to come and see her."

"But he's more than eleven hundred kilometres away." Mr Edwards was at another country school, and he was very surprised when he received a long-distance phone call from Mr Swan.

"Mr Edwards, there's a little Aborigine girl here. She's nine years old. You *must* come and see her."

Mr Edwards thought eleven hundred kilometres was a very long way to travel in order to see a little girl of nine. He felt a little annoyed. He also felt rather curious, so he took the next plane to Barellan to watch Evonne.

"Yes," he told Mrs Martin. "She certainly has something special. Yes, she certainly ought to have good training all the year round, but how can she get that in Barellan? You say her parents are very poor, with a big family to look after. How could they possibly afford to pay for her training anyway, even if she could go to Sydney?"

"But she's the most promising child I've ever seen," protested Mrs Martin. "We ought to do *something* about her."

Mr Edwards was a kind man.

"I'll talk to Mr Kurtzman about her," he said, "and I'll talk to my wife when I get back home. Maybe we can work something out between us."

So a plan was made. Evonne was invited to fly to Sydney during the school holiday at the end of May, to stay with the Edwards family for two weeks. There she would get to know the Edwards girls, Jenifer, aged eleven and Trisha, nine. Mr Edwards would give her daily tennis coaching and she could take part in the tournaments that were held in Sydney at that time of year. She could stay with the Edwards for two weeks every Easter, two weeks every May, and eight weeks during the long Christmas (summer) holidays.

That was the plan, but would it work? Evonne was a country girl. Barellan was a quiet little town, where everything moved slowly. Sydney was such a big city, with its noisy streets and its skyscrapers and its great

bridge across the harbour. When Evonne first arrived there she wondered if she would ever be able to bear it. It was so far from home. It was so different. She missed her mother and father and brothers and sisters so much. She was only nine years old, and she was very homesick.

. . . .

Evonne had two families now. She had her own mother and father and brothers and sisters in Barellan, and she had Mr and Mrs Edwards and Jenifer and Trisha in Sydney. She was often homesick over the years, but at the same time she settled happily during holidays in Sydney, and became great friends with Trisha, whose room she shared.

She played tennis. She had hard, daily coaching at Mr Edwards's school. She practised, she practised. She won most of her tournaments. In Sydney she had no escape from tennis, but fortunately she never wanted to escape. She just went on, working hard, getting better and better. She was happy when she played, so that she made the people who watched her feel happy too. She smiled if she were winning. She smiled if she were losing. If she won a game she was pleased. If she lost, well, it didn't matter. It was only a game. Why get all worked up and unhappy about a game?

. . . . . .

Then when Evonne was thirteen, kind Mr Kurtzman started worrying about her again. He had become very fond of this little Aborigine girl. He was proud of her too. The holiday arrangement seemed to be working out well, but it was not enough. Evonne had the ability to become an Australian tennis star, but she needed

more than holiday training three times a year. Mr Edwards knew this too. Probably every tennis coach dreams of training a champion – someone who will win and win and win, and go at last to Wimbledon to win there. Perhaps Mr Edwards had these dreams about Evonne.

So a new plan was made. Evonne was to move right in with the Edwards family. She was to go to school with Jenifer and Trisha in Sydney. She would be able to have all the tennis coaching that Mr Edwards and his teachers could give her. She would be trained for big, important games against top Australian players and then for games against top world players.

Mr Kurtzman talked to the people of Barellan. They were willing to help towards living expenses and air fares. Hundreds of people gave a little money every year to help Evonne on her way.

. . . . . .

It was 1971. In England it was summer and daylight. In Barellan, Australia, it was dark and after midnight, but everyone who had a television was sitting in front of it, and people who had no television were sitting in front of those belonging to neighbours. Evonne was playing at Wimbledon. She was nineteen now, and she had come through the semi-finals and reached the final.

She was playing Margaret Court, another Australian champion, so Australia was going to win in any case. But the people of Barellan wanted Evonne to win – Evonne, the little Aborigine girl they had helped and supported from the beginning.

They watched her darting across the screen with her strong strokes and her quick and beautiful movements. Her dark, curly hair was damp with perspiration and she

was smiling, as always. She was winning. Then her score slipped back to deuce. She and Margaret were even again. It was Margaret's service now. She missed. She served again. A double fault. Evonne had won. Evonne was the new Wimbledon champion – the new world champion.

The people of Barellan were overcome with pride and pleasure. Now they were watching Evonne giving a little curtsey to Princess Alexandra on the other side of the world. Now they were watching her receive the great gold platter and raise it above her head to show the clapping, cheering crowd.

Evonne Goolagong from Barellan, in Australia, had come a long way.

. . . . . .

Much of the information in this story is taken from the book *Evonne* by Evonne Goolagong and Bud Collins, published by Hart-Davis, MacGibbon.

Small Stories – 2

1. Benjamin Franklin was a famous American. He was a scientist and a politician. He invented the lightning conductor. He made a special fireplace or stove that would prevent smoky chimneys. He thought of having town streets paved in order to keep them cleaner. He invented fire companies, which we now know as "fire insurance" companies. He helped to write America's Declaration of Independence in 1776. While working on this and changing the wording of Thomas Jefferson, he told the following story:

A man called John Thompson was planning to start a hatter's shop, and he drew a rough plan of a notice board to hang above the door. He drew a picture of a hat, and wrote,

"John Thompson, hatter, makes and sells hats for ready money". He showed it to a friend, saying,

"What do you think of this?"

"I should cross out the word 'hatter'," was the reply. "You've put 'makes hats'. That shows you're a hatter." So John Thompson crossed out "hatter", and showed the notice to a second friend. This friend said,

"People won't care who makes the hats. I should cross out 'makes'." John Thompson did so. He also crossed out "and". The notice now read,

"John Thompson sells hats for ready money".

A third friend pointed out that anyone who went in the shop to buy a hat would of course expect to pay for it.

"Cross out 'for ready money'," he suggested. John Thompson did so. Now the notice read,

"John Thompson sells hats".

"Why 'sells'?" asked a family friend. "No one will expect you to give hats away." So John Thompson crossed out "sells" and left only,

"John Thompson. Hats".

"You don't need to write 'hats'," advised someone else. "The picture is enough."

So the notice ended up with only the name "John Thompson" with a picture of a hat beside it.

2. Demosthenes was a famous Greek teacher and politician. One day he was speaking to the people of Athens about something important to city life. They showed so little interest in what he was saying, that he felt very angry. He suddenly changed his tone of voice and began to tell a story instead.

"One very hot day," he said, "a young man hired a donkey. He led it away, walking in its shadow to keep cool. The owner of the donkey called after him,

'You hired the donkey from me, but you did not hire its shadow.' The young man turned round and replied—"

Demosthenes stopped speaking and began to walk home, but the people wanted to know what happened next. They followed him, saying,

"What happened next? What did the young man say?" Demosthenes answered angrily,

"When I tell you a foolish story about the shadow of a donkey, you want me to go on with it, but when I try to tell you something important, you refuse to listen."

Jet Flight

From quite an early age, Frank Whittle knew what he wanted to do. He wanted to work with aeroplanes. He wanted to make them, improve them, design them, and most of all, to fly them.

Aeroplanes were fairly new in those days, for Frank was born in 1907, only four years after the Wright brothers had started their historic flights. So, as Frank grew, aeroplanes were growing too. They were becoming less clumsy. They were reaching greater heights and greater speeds, and travelling greater distances.

As a small boy, he drew numerous pictures of them. As a bigger boy, he spent many hours in the local library studying the theory of flight, and reading books on engineering and practical flying. He studied the subject so much that he felt quite sure he would be able to fly without having any actual teaching.

His father had been employed in a cotton mill at the age of eleven, but he had worked hard through his life and had saved up enough money to start a small, one-man engineering factory. He was a skilful mechanic, and very inventive. He made small parts for cars, machines, guns, and sometimes even for aeroplanes. Frank liked to help him in his workshop. He asked many questions, and learned to use the different tools; and by the time he was ten, he had become quite skilful. Then his father allowed him to make some of the things he needed for his orders, and he paid him for his work.

At that time, the Royal Air Force had started a scheme for training boys to work with planes. They could start as apprentices at the age of fifteen or sixteen, learning as they worked. They would learn to build aeroplanes, and to repair and maintain them. Then at the end of three years, there would be a chance for some of the boys to join the Flight Cadet Wing. They would be taught to fly, and in two more years would become pilots. What could be better?

When Frank became fifteen years old, there was no need for his parents to ask him what he wanted to do when he left school. They knew. He wanted to join the Royal Air Force, and the best way to go about it seemed to be to start as an aircraft apprentice. There was an entrance examination to take, but this did not worry

Frank too much. He had always worked reasonably well at school, and he had stored up a great deal of knowledge from library books. He took the exam at Halton Royal Air Force station. Then he waited eagerly and anxiously for the results.

One day not long afterwards, a letter came for him with the magic sign upon it. He tore it open and read it.

"I've passed! I've passed!" he exclaimed to his parents in relief. Then he read the letter again and added, "Just a medical exam to take now. That should be easy enough. I've always been strong and healthy."

A few days later, he reported to the doctor at the R.A.F. station. The doctor sounded his chest, tested his sight and hearing, asked a number of questions, weighed and measured him. Frank was quite sure that everything was all right, and he looked up expectantly for the doctor's verdict.

"I'm sorry," said the doctor, "but I can't pass you."

"Can't pass me!" Frank could hardly believe it. "But why not?" he asked. "I'm strong and healthy. I'm never ill."

"It's your height," explained the doctor. "You're only one and a half metres. That's not tall enough for the R.A.F." Frank's heart sank. Height! What had height to do with flying aeroplanes? What had height to do with making them and maintaining them?

"You're undersized too," went on the doctor. "Your weight is low, and your chest measurement isn't up to standard."

In a daze, Frank stumbled out of the room. Not tall enough. Not broad enough. Not heavy enough.

He had always been a small boy. He knew that, of course, but he was strong and wiry. He could run and jump and climb a great deal faster and higher than most of his taller and bigger friends.

What did height have to do with it?

All his dreams were shattered, but he would not give up hope – not yet. He stayed around the R.A.F. station. He spoke to one or two men. Wasn't there any other way of getting accepted? No, no other way.

Then a physical training instructor spoke to him. His name was Sergeant Holmes. He could see that Frank was unhappy. Perhaps he guessed what was wrong.

"Didn't you pass the medical?" he asked.

"No. I'm not tall enough."

"Bad luck! Still, there are other things in life besides flying." There might be, but Frank wanted to fly.

Sergeant Holmes was a kind man.

"How old are you?" he asked.

"Fifteen."

"Fifteen's nothing. You'll grow a lot more yet."

"Yes, but –"

"I know. You need to grow at once. I tell you what. I'll show you some body-building exercises, and I'll give you a diet sheet. Come in here."

A little later, Frank left the Halton Air Force station with a list of exercises, and a list of suitable things to eat. His mother had always given him nourishing meals, but the list showed the things that would most likely help to build up height and weight.

"I'll pass next time," thought Frank grimly, and almost as soon as he reached home, he started working hard. His mother helped with the right meals; and day by day Frank did the exercises. He did not really enjoy

doing them, but he was determined to increase his height and expand his chest. Day after day, week after week, he followed Sergeant Holmes's plan.

Then in six months' time, he measured himself again. He measured his chest with his mother's tape measure. He measured his height against a chalk mark he had made on the outside wall of his house. The results were better than he had dared to hope! In six months he had put on eight centimetres round his chest, and had added eight centimetres to his height!

"I'm taller!" he said proudly to his parents. "Now I'll ask to take the medical exam again."

He wrote a letter to the Halton R.A.F. station, explaining what had happened, but when the reply came, it dashed his hopes once more.

"We regret that applicants are not allowed a second chance," it said. A failure was a failure. The results were final.

For a few days, Frank was in despair. Then he wrote again. He explained that he had passed the written examination, but had failed the medical because he had not reached the required height and weight. He explained that he had now added eight centimetres to his height and to his chest measurement.

"I am very keen to become an aircraft apprentice," he added. "Will you please reconsider my case." Again the answer was no.

Then Frank had a brilliant idea.

"Halton isn't the only R.A.F. station in England," he said excitedly to his parents. "There are several others. I'll apply to another one. I'll start all over again. They'll never compare the application forms of different stations with each other."

"Good idea," agreed his father.

"What about the doctor?" asked his mother, a little doubtfully. "It's possible that he goes from station to station."

"Oh, that would be bad luck," said Father, "but I hardly think Frank would get the same one."

Frank looked at his list of R.A.F stations, and picked out Cranwell. It was a well-known training college for pilots and air force officers, and it had a school for aircraft apprentices. He sent for the application form, filled it in and returned it. No one at Cranwell knew that Frank Whittle had been rejected at Halton. He was invited to take the entrance examination at Cranwell. He passed it.

"Now for the medical," he said, as he had said once before.

This time he felt rather nervous. Would he, by some awful chance, have to face the same doctor?

No. It was a different doctor. Frank breathed a sigh

of relief. All the same, he was glad when it was all over – the questions, the tests of sight and hearing, the weighing, the measuring.

"Fine," said the doctor. "Nothing wrong there."

Frank had passed. No one knew he had applied to the R.A.F. twice. No one ever would know unless he told them. He was sixteen now, and he was accepted as one of the six hundred aircraft apprentices at Cranwell. In September 1923 he started his training.

· · · · · ·

At that time, wood was giving way to metal in aircraft construction. So it was in this type of aeroplane building that Frank received his early training. Part of every week was spent in the workshop, and part in lessons

similar to those of a school. There was also a certain amount of physical training and drill as there was in the army. Frank enjoyed much of the life, and the companionship of other apprentices, but there were often times when he felt bored and impatient. He still seemed a long way from actually flying. Meanwhile, he joined the Model Aircraft Society. This gave him an outlet for his ideas and his imagination. It also taught him more about flight.

He disliked the army-type discipline and the drill and the marching and the Saturday morning parades. On these parades, as he stood or marched with the Apprentices' Wing, he always gazed in envy at the Flight Cadet Wing. The cadets were always smarter and nearer perfection than anyone else. They were the men who actually spent their time learning to fly, and actually counting the hours they flew solo. All through the three years, Frank hoped and longed to join them.

Then at last came the final exams. Only five apprentices were to be chosen to join the Flight Cadet Wing. They would be the top five. Frank, to his great disappointment, came sixth. He had missed the chance by one place, and probably his marks were only slightly lower than the men above him.

Then a little luck came his way. It was bad luck for someone else, but good luck for him. One of the five top apprentices failed the medical test, so Frank was given his place. To his delight, he became a member of the Flight Cadet Wing. In his second term he flew solo for the first time. This was what he had waited for. It was sheer joy.

· · · · · ·

As Frank's hours of solo flying increased, so did the development of his thoughts and ideas on future and better aeroplanes. In those days, R.A.F. fighter planes could reach a speed of 240 kilometres an hour. Frank dreamed of flying at 800 kilometres an hour. He knew, however, that if this speed were ever to be reached, aeroplanes would have to fly at much greater heights, where the air resistance would be less. The ordinary piston engine and propeller would never provide the necessary force for high speeds and long distances. There must be a better way.

When he completed his two-year course in the Flight Cadet Wing at Cranwell in 1928, he knew that he would no longer be content to be a pilot only. He would design aircraft too.

· · · · · ·

For years, Frank Whittle battled with the problem of making a new sort of engine for larger, faster aircraft.

Looking back on the history of flight, he found that in 1917 a man called Dr Harris had suggested a jet-propelled engine. A strong jet of air was to be sucked in at the front of the plane and forced out at the back. This would push the machine forward. It seemed a good idea, but it was very expensive and had not been thought good enough to put into use.

Whittle now took up this idea afresh. He developed it, and introduced a gas turbine to create a stronger, faster jet. He knew he was now on the way to success.

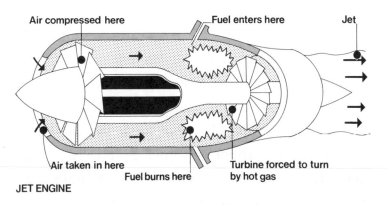

JET ENGINE

The way of an inventor is nearly always hard. First he has to find someone who has faith in his invention. Then he has to find someone who will provide the money to pay for it to be tried out. After that, there are many long experiments and trials. There are many mistakes and breakdowns and improvements and more improvements.

Frank worked and worked on his development of the turbo-jet. He worked and struggled for years and years, and it was not until 1941 that his own Meteor plane streaked its way into the news with successful test flights. It had no pistons or propeller. It was driven by turbo-jet. It reached a speed of five hundred and ninety kilometres an hour at a height of seven thousand five hundred metres.

Today nearly all the larger and faster planes are driven by jet; and all jet aircraft are based on the hard work, imagination and perseverance of Frank Whittle.

The facts in this story are taken from Sir Frank Whittle's book, *Jet*, published by Frederick Muller Ltd.

Juliane in the Jungle

Juliane lived in the city of Lima in Peru. Her mother and father taught in the university, but they and Juliane often spent long holidays in the jungle. There they had a simple hut where they lived and worked, studying birds and plants and insects and small animals. To reach the jungle they had to fly over the Andes Mountains to a town called Pucallpa. It was quite a short flight. It took only about an hour and a quarter, and the plane left at regular times from Lima.

It was lonely in the jungle, but Juliane took books to read and sometimes some school work to do. She was interested too in the animals and birds and plants, and she helped her parents with their notes and studies.

They taught her a lot about the jungle. They taught her which plants could be used for food, and which were poisonous. They taught her which creatures were harmless, and which were dangerous.

"It's not the big animals you have to fear so much as the small ones," her father explained. "It's the deadly snakes, the stinging insects and the poisonous spiders, and the little worms that dig into your flesh."

He also told her what to do if she were lost.

"There are no roads in the jungle," he said, "but there are rivers. In places, there are white people and tribes of Indians living on the banks. If you just walk on and on, you might walk in circles for days. Remember Juliane, if you ever get lost, look for a stream and follow it. Follow it until it runs into a bigger stream. Then follow that until it meets a river. Then follow the river and sooner or later you will come to people."

"I'll remember," said Juliane. However, there was not much chance of being lost in the jungle. Juliane never walked into it without one of her parents, and most of their work was done quite near to the hut. They had cleared a small patch of ground around it, but beyond that, like a green curtain, was a thick tangle of trees and vines and long swaying creepers. There were clusters of pink and yellow orchids clinging to twigs and branches. There were giant ferns and bright fallen flowers and a mass of jumbled greenery on the forest floor. Sometimes the jungle was silent and full of secrets, but at certain times of day brilliant birds would dart about, shrieking and calling; and monkeys would chatter and shout to each other in the distance. Holidays for Juliane meant the jungle.

Then came the Christmas holiday when she was seventeen years old. School had broken up rather late and Mother and Father were already settled in the jungle hut. It was Juliane's last term at school, and she was waiting now to fly out and join her parents.

It was the day before Christmas, and she sat by the window in the Electra plane belonging to the Lansa airline. It was hot summer weather and she was wearing a cotton frock. She was one of ninety-two passengers.

The aeroplane rose in the air, and Lima was spread out below. Juliane looked down at its streets and squares and trees and fountains. Higher rose the plane, and higher. Soon it was flying over the Andes, where the sun

gleamed and sparkled on the snowy peaks. A late breakfast was served on the plane – a cup of coffee, with crisp rolls and butter and jam fitted neatly in separate spaces on a plastic tray. It all helped to pass the time. Juliane looked at her watch. Already half an hour had gone. Already the Andes Mountains were lost in the distance, and the plane was over the jungle.

There it was far below, damp and green like a misty sea. Soon the sun disappeared and rain began to fall. It splashed against the windows, and ran down the glass in small swift streams.

"What a pity," thought Juliane. "It's usually such a beautiful flight."

A stewardess came round to collect the empty breakfast trays. The plane was shaking and tossing now like

a ship on a rough sea. The stewardess had a job to walk straight. A small case fell down from a rack. The plane shook and lurched and seemed almost out of control.

Juliane felt a little afraid. Then a vivid flash of lightning made her cringe back from the window and close her eyes. A second later, as she opened them, she saw a brilliant yellow flame leap from the wing of the aeroplane. Something terrible had happened. Had the plane been struck by lightning? Had it exploded?

She would never know, for next moment Juliane found herself flying through the air as if in some awful nightmare. She was still held in her seat by the safety strap. She was turning over and over as she fell down and down towards the green jungle below. Where was the aeroplane? It was nowhere to be seen. Where were the other passengers? There was no one in sight.

Juliane remembered nothing more until evening, when she awoke to the sound of dripping rain and croaking frogs. She was lying on the ground with a row of three aeroplane seats resting on top of her. One of her eyes was swollen and almost closed. She had banged her head and hurt her neck, and she had a deep cut in her foot. She had lost her glasses and her shoes. She was too weak and shocked to move. She lay where she was, and dozed on and off through the night.

In the morning she was awakened by the cries of the jungle – parrots screaming, monkeys calling. For one brief moment she thought she was on holiday in the hut. Then she remembered, and her heart sank. She crept out from under the seats and lay for a while on a tangled mass of plants. She saw a box in front of her. She opened it. It was full of sweets.

"These might be useful," she thought. She picked up a long stick, and tried to stand, but she felt so dizzy that she sank to the ground again.

After a while she tried once more. She felt as if everything was spinning round her, but she managed to take a few slow steps. With one hand, she clutched the box of sweets. With the other, she poked about in front of her with the stick, to clear the way of snakes or deadly insects. Sharp stems and leaves pricked her bare feet. Ants and small beetles crawled over them. Where were the other people? Where was the aeroplane?

She stumbled on dizzily, stopping often to rest. She came upon a piece of twisted metal and three plane seats fixed together. She came upon a blackened patch of ground that smelled strongly of burning. Then she heard the sound of water. There was a little stream! She remembered her father saying,

"Remember Juliane, if you are ever lost in the jungle, look for a stream and follow it." Gladly she followed the stream. It was not at all easy, because the banks were thick with plants, and there were sometimes fallen tree trunks lying in her way.

Slowly she pressed onwards, hoping and hoping that the stream would flow into a river, and she would find people to help her, and to search for the other passengers. Meanwhile insects stung her face again and again, and flies began to lay eggs in the deep cut in her foot.

Once she heard an aeroplane high above the trees. Perhaps it was looking for the crashed aircraft. She stood still and shouted, "Help! Help!" But no one heard her. She could not even see the plane, so how could she expect the pilot to see her? Bravely she walked on. Now and again she ate a few sweets from the box. Now and again she drank water from the stream. Her journey was very slow. Straggling plants twisted themselves round her ankles. Hordes of ants walked across her path. A snake slithered by. Big toads jumped and flopped around her. Horrid little maggots began to crawl about in the deep cut in her foot. Mosquitoes buzzed around her and stung her again and again and again. Days passed. Nights passed.

It was all like a bad dream, but if the days were bad, the nights were even worse. Darkness always came suddenly. Juliane tried hard to sleep, but there were so many rustling sounds and small movements, so many creepy, crawly feelings on her legs and arms. There were so many little moments of fear that sometimes sleep came to her hardly at all.

When the sun rose in the mornings she would stand up wearily and walk onwards. At last one day she reached a place where the stream flowed into a river. This gave her new hope, and she followed the river downstream. Perhaps she would soon find people living on its banks.

The air was very hot and damp. Juliane finished the sweets. She had nothing at all to eat now, and she dare not try any of the fruit that looked so tempting. She saw monkeys swinging in the trees and brightly coloured parrots flying past. She saw beautiful little humming birds sucking honey from jungle flowers.

She grew weaker and slower each day, but sometimes she swam in the river for short distances. She knew it was dangerous, for there were fish that might attack her wounded foot with their cruel jaws, but the current was strong and carried her along swiftly.

The wound in her foot was growing worse, as the horrid little maggots ate away the flesh. More flies settled and laid more eggs. More little maggots hatched out to eat her flesh. Sometimes Juliane could not

manage to walk more than a few hundred metres a day, and now the river was flowing too fast for swimming. Sometimes she wondered if she would ever reach safety.

Days and nights passed and she lost all count of them. On the tenth day she was stumbling along in a tangle of rotting leaves, looking for a place to lie down for the night when suddenly she saw something that made her heart thump with relief. A boat! There was a boat tied to a tree on the bank of the river. If there was a boat, there must be people somewhere near. Juliane looked round and saw a little hut. She knocked on the door but there was no one about. She pushed open the door and entered the hut. There was a can of petrol and an outboard motor standing inside. Soon, someone would come to fetch them. But when?

Juliane stretched herself out on the floor. Darkness fell. There were rustlings and movements outside the hut. What were they? Juliane hoped and hoped to hear human footsteps, human voices, but none came. She slept and woke and slept and woke. The night passed at last and it was morning again.

"What shall I do?" thought Juliane. "Shall I take the boat? It would be much quicker than walking. No, I can't do that. It's not mine to take. Shall I wait here till its owners come back for it? No, it might be weeks before they come. I'd better struggle on."

She looked out of the door, but now it was raining. Rain was beating down on the straggling plants and the thirsty trees. It was splashing on the river in a thousand tiny fountains.

"I'd better wait a little while," said Juliane to herself. She sat on the floor and tried to dig some of the maggots out of her foot with a small, sharp piece of palm wood. She scarcely felt the pain, just as she scarcely felt hunger even after all this time. She just felt weak, terribly, terribly weak.

Suddenly there were voices. The door burst open and three men hurried in out of the rain.

"What's this?" they exclaimed in surprise. They were hunters, partly white and partly Indian. They spoke Spanish. They were kind and helpful. They washed Juliane's torn and scratched legs and arms. They dug out lots of the maggots, and put ointment on the wounds. They bandaged her foot and mashed up some fruit for her to eat. She tried hard, but she could not swallow it.

"So you're from the aeroplane that crashed!" said one of the men. "I actually flew over the jungle in a rescue plane looking for it. We couldn't find anything. We couldn't find the machine or any parts of it. We couldn't see any people, or –"

Juliane's head swayed, and the truth began to dawn

on her. No one else had been saved. She must be the only one of the ninety-two passengers left alive.

· · · · · · ·

The next day the three men took Juliane in their boat to the nearest jungle settlement. It took many hours. Juliane looked at the banks as the boat passed. She saw how difficult it would have been for her to walk along it. It would have taken her days and days. She might never have come out of the jungle alive.

Nor might she have come out alive if the rain had not kept her waiting a little while in the hut – till the moment when the men had arrived there. That too was a miracle, for they visited the hut only once in three weeks – and they had come just at the right time for her.

When they reached the jungle settlement, Juliane was given medical attention and flown to Pucallpa, where she was taken to hospital. Her eyes were red and bloodshot, and her face was swollen out of shape with all the insect bites. Her arms and legs were covered in cuts and scratches and there were numerous little holes and tunnels dug by worms. The wound in her foot was deep and dangerous, but in time it would heal. In time too, her health and strength would return. Meanwhile she was just thankful to be alive.

Adapted by courtesy of "Stern" Magazine

News of Dinosaurs and Others

Evidence of dinosaurs and other ancient creatures is still being found. In the nineteen-seventies the following were discovered:

A workman in some English gravel pits found a skull nearly a metre long. It belonged to a woolly rhinoceros that walked the earth at least thirty thousand years ago.

A nest of baby dinosaurs was found on an American ranch. There were fifteen babies. They were nearly three-quarters of a metre long and twenty-five centimetres high. They were plant-eating hadrosaurs with duck-shaped bills, and they would have grown to a length of about nine or ten metres. They lived about seventy to seventy-five million years ago.

In Western Queensland, Australia, tracks were found on a hill, showing that a big dinosaur had attacked a herd of about sixty smaller ones. The battle must have taken place about a hundred million years ago.

The oldest known flying creature in the world left the imprint of its wing on a piece of coal which was found nine hundred metres underground. The wing was more than twenty centimetres long, and belonged to a dragon-fly that lived three hundred million years ago.

. . . . . .

Some dinosaurs weighed thirty tonnes. Yet they found enough food to keep their race surviving on earth for a hundred and forty million years. Then about sixty-four million years ago they died out or disappeared. Why?

There are several theories. Here are four of them:
1 They could not stand a change to icy cold weather.
2 They could not stand a change to burning hot weather.
3 Their brains grew too big.
4 They were conquered by little rodents like shrews or small rats. These tiny creatures multiplied very quickly and scuttled hither and thither, eating the available food supply from under the very noses of the heavy, slower dinosaurs.

A Stitch in the Air

It was 1872, the year of a terrible winter in Venice. It was bad enough for the city itself, but it was even worse for the little islands in the lagoon; and for Burano it was the worst of all.

The men of Burano made their living by fishing, but that winter they were kept at home by storms and wild winds. Then mists and snow showers swirled above the island, and the waters froze around its shores. The little rowing boats and sailing boats were held tightly in the grip of ice. The families in the rows of brightly-painted houses had nothing to keep themselves warm, except small oil lamps and little bronze pots of glowing charcoal. Everyone was cold, and as days and weeks went by, everyone was hungry too.

The children played as usual. They ran and slid in the square where the tall, crooked bell-tower stood. They chased each other up and down the narrow paths beside canals where water usually flowed, and moored boats usually swayed up and down. Then soon they stopped playing because they were so hungry and they had not much energy left.

"The people of Burano must be starving," said the Italians on the mainland. "They cannot go fishing.

They cannot get supplies of food, and they are always very poor anyway."

The news came to the ears of the Pope and the King of Italy.

"The lagoon is a sheet of ice. The people on the island of Burano must be starving."

The Pope and the King started a fund to help the islanders. People all over the country gave what they could afford. Concerts were held, to raise money. Theatres put on special plays and operas, and gave all the ticket money to the fund.

"As soon as the ice begins to break up, we will send food supplies to Burano," said the Italians.

A great deal of money was collected. It was more than enough to buy all that was needed. As soon as the ice began to thaw and break up, boats set out from Venice to Burano. There were big, open boats stacked with wood for cooking. There were boats laden with food.

By the time the last of the ice had melted or drifted away on the tide, everything was back to normal. The people were no longer hungry. The air was warmer. A pale sun peeped through the grey clouds. Spring came. The men went fishing. The children played again.

But on the mainland, the people who had collected the money held a meeting.

"There is a large sum left over. What shall we do with it?" they asked each other.

"It was given for Burano. We must think of the best way of using it."

"It seems to me," said someone, "that there ought to be another way for the people to earn their living, instead of depending only on fishing. Fishing depends on the weather. The families could be hungry again at any time, and they are always very poor."

Then one man had an idea.

"Burano used to be famous for lace-making," he said. "The women used to do it in their own homes and sell it."

"Yes, that's right. Burano lace was famous for hundreds of years. There was a school of lace-making there once. Orders for lace used to come from many parts of the world."

"It all died out a long time ago," said someone else. "Fashions changed."

"But lace is still used for altar cloths and church robes; and some people still like it on tablecloths and blouses and collars."

"Couldn't we start the women of Burano on lace-making again? We could open a small school. We have the money."

Everyone thought it was a good idea. Then one of the women at the meeting said,

"But Burano lace was made in a special way. It was not made by passing bobbins from side to side and making knotted patterns, as with ordinary lace. Burano lace was all done with a needle. It was so fine and delicate that it had the name of 'A Stitch in the Air.' I have not seen any for many years. I wonder if there is anyone left now who knows the secret of making it."

"We will look for someone."

A few days later, the people of Burano were surprised to see two richly-dressed ladies walking in their narrow streets. They came from Venice, and one of them was the Countess Adriana. It was a sunny day, and some of the women of the island were sitting in their doorways, sewing or mending. Others were chatting to each other, so glad that the winter had passed at last.

The countess went up to a little group.

"Can any of you make lace?" she asked.

"Oh yes Madam, I can make it," replied one woman.

"How do you make it?" asked the countess.

"I make it on a pillow with pins and little bobbins and fine cotton."

"Do you know how to make the special Burano lace called 'A Stitch in the Air'?"

"Oh no Madam. I have heard my mother speak of it, but even she does not know how it was made."

The countess moved on towards other women. She asked the same questions,

"Can you make lace?"

"How do you make it?"

"Do you know how to make the special Burano lace called 'A Stitch in the Air'?"

Several women knew how to make ordinary lace on a pillow, with pins and little bobbins and fine cotton, but no one knew how to make the fine, delicate lace

called "A Stitch in the Air". Some said they would ask their mothers or their grandmothers, but even they did not know the secret.

Then at last, someone brought an old lady to the countess. Her name was Cencia. She said that her grandmother had made the "Stitch in the Air" lace long ago.

"She taught me how to do it when I was a little girl, but I have never made it since."

"Do you think you could remember how to do it?" asked the Countess.

"I could try Madam."

So Cencia was made comfortable on a chair in the sun. She was given a small, hard cushion to rest in her lap. She was given fine cotton and a needle. A little group of women gathered round her to watch. At first she could not remember. Then as her mind went back to the days of her childhood, it suddenly came to her. Old people sometimes cannot remember things that have happened just a day or two before, but they often have very clear pictures in their minds of things that happened when they were young. It was like that now, with Cencia.

"I remember," she said. "We used to work the pattern on a piece of cloth. Then when the lace was finished, we used to cut the cloth right away so that the lace was left in the air. It will take me a few days, but I think I shall be able to do it."

A few days later, when the Countess Adriana came to Burano again, the old lady, Cencia, had a piece of lace to show her. It was beautifully worked with a needle. It was made with tiny, tiny stitches and little raised flowers and leaves. It was fine and delicate, almost like gossamer. It was real "Stitch in the Air".

So a lace-making school was started once more in Burano. One or two teachers watched Cencia over and over again. Then when they had learned the method, they taught it to others. The school began with eight pupils, and it grew bigger and bigger. "Stitch in the Air" lace was sold to tourists, and ordered by many cities for churches or shops. In 1880 the lace earned 34 327 lire (lire are Italian coins) for the island. In 1906 it earned 154 802 lire. So it kept hunger and poverty away from Burano for the next hundred years.

Once Upon a Time

When you were five or six years old, you probably heard the story of Rumpelstiltskin for the first time. "Once upon a time there lived a poor miller who had a beautiful daughter . . ." You may remember that the miller was so proud of his daughter that he told the king she could spin straw into gold. So the king put her into a room full of straw and told her to spin it into gold by the morning. She wept because she could not do it, and a little man appeared and helped her. He spun all the straw into gold for three nights running. The girl gave him her necklace and her ring, but on the third night she had nothing left to give, so she foolishly made a promise. She agreed that if ever she became queen (which seemed very unlikely) she would give the little man her first-born child.

In time, she did become queen and she gave birth to a child. The little man appeared and reminded her of her promise, but the girl wept so bitterly that at last he said she could keep the baby on one condition. She had to guess the little man's name. For two nights, the queen tried all the names she could think of, or invent. But by the third night a messenger had brought her news of the real name and after a while she said slowly,

"Could your name be Rumpelstiltskin?"

So the story ended happily and perhaps you heard it again and again. Then one day you read the same story, or almost the same story, but this time the little man had a different name. He was called Tom-Tit-Tot. You may even have seen the name as Trit-a-Trot or Whuppity Stoorie. Why? Why couldn't people tell the story properly, you thought.

The fact is, that people in so many different countries have thought of the story as their own, that they have given their own names to the little man, and made their own small changes here and there. The story was told many, many times before it was ever written down. It passed from parent to child, parent to child, through great-grandmothers and great-great-grandmothers. It seemed as if it started in lots of different countries at once. It is what we call a "folk-tale", and no one can tell where or when it began.

Children in Spain know the story. Children in Scandinavia know it. Children hear it in Russia, Italy, Hungary, Austria. French children call the little man Ricdin-Ricdon. Irish children call him Trit-a-Trot. Children in Iceland call him Gilitrutt. Scottish children think of him as a fairy woman, called Whuppity Stoorie. Welsh children have two or three names. England itself has more than one name – Terry Top in Cornwall, Tom-Tit-Tot in Suffolk. So the story goes on down the ages – a little different here and there, but always the same task – "If you can guess my name, you may keep your baby."

Now think of Little Red Riding Hood. You have known her since you were very young. But did she and her poor grandmother end up in the wolf's stomach? Or did a forester, or Little Red Riding Hood's father, shoot the wolf just before it ate the child? And did the grandmother then appear from a cupboard where she had hidden in time to save herself? Or did a forester, or Little Red Riding Hood's father, find the wolf sleeping in bed, and did they cut him open and let out the grandmother and the child, unharmed?

Rumpelstiltskin and Little Red Riding Hood seem to belong to the western world, but many of the other stories you read are much, much older and are told in slightly different forms in Africa, India, America and countries and islands scattered all over the world.

The most popular story in the world is "Cinderella". There are (if you can imagine it) seven hundred slightly different Cinderella stories. Each one begins with a good, sweet girl who is treated unkindly and made to do all the work in the house.

Most of the stories bring in someone with magic powers, who gives Cinderella beautiful clothes and slippers. In England it is a fairy godmother, but in other countries it is usually an animal of some kind. It may be an ox, a calf, a wolf, a cow, a mouse, a toad, a bird or even a fish or an eel. The stories end with Cinderella trying on the slipper (or sometimes a ring) and marrying the Prince. The slipper may be made of straw, velvet, silk, gold, fur or glass, but it must fit perfectly.

One of the earliest written versions came from China in the ninth century A.D., but it had no doubt been told long before that. The story is found in Asia, Africa, America, Europe, Scandinavia; and in the year eighteen hundred and ninety-two, a lady called Marion Cox published a book containing more than three hundred versions of Cinderella from many different countries.

No one can possibly know when most of the folk stories were first told. Their beginnings are lost in the mists of the far distant past. Mothers told them to children. Story-tellers told them to groups of people in their villages. The magic has gone on from century to century. It must have been hundreds, even thousands, of years before some of the stories were written down. It is fairly certain though that the first *written* accounts of the stories came from the East. We can meet Puss in Boots in a collection of folk-tales written down in India in the third century A.D. We are introduced to the "Princess on the Pea" in India in the ninth century.

In Europe, it was an Italian who first set some of the stories down in writing, about the year 1550. This was followed by a better-known Italian collection written in Naples by a man called Basile. He was a soldier, a poet and finally governor of his district. The stories filled five volumes, printed between 1634 and 1636, and Basile had probably heard them from women in the market place, women at the wells, cobblers in the squares, fishermen on the beaches. In Basile's books we meet Puss in Boots again. We also meet Cinderella, Beauty and the Beast, Snow White and the Sleeping Beauty.

Then at the beginning of the year 1697 a book appeared in Paris written by an elderly civil servant named Charles Perrault. He was a handsome man with an enormous curled wig like those worn by Louis XIV, the King of France. Perrault's "Stories of Past Times" included among others, Little Red Riding Hood, the Sleeping Beauty, Puss in Boots, Cinderella, Hop o' my Thumb. He had heard his small son's old nurse telling the stories, and he had probably never read Basile's Italian book.

Perrault wrote other books on more learned subjects, but it was his "fairy tales" that made him famous. The rich nobles and ladies at the court of Louis XIV were delighted with their simplicity and freshness. So, stories which might have been lost and forgotten had been saved for all the children of the future. In 1729 Perrault's stories were translated into English and became some of the most often repeated and best known in the language.

There were other people who saved stories, or told them in different ways, but the most famous of all the story collectors were the brothers Jacob and Wilhelm Grimm. They lived in Germany, which in those days was a number of separate states. Jacob was born in January 1785 and Wilhelm in February a year later. They were the eldest of a family of six children and they lived in a pleasant house near a tower where a pair of storks nested every year. Around their village were woods and fields. Their childhood was happy. The family were close and loving, but Jacob and Wilhelm were especially fond of each other and worked together throughout most of their lives.

When they were children they shared a room, a bed, and a table. When they were students they had two beds and two tables in the same room. Then they worked in rooms next to each other in the same house. They shared their books and their belongings; and when Wilhelm married, he still shared a house with his brother. Even his children were shared as well.

The Grimm brothers were quiet, clever, hard-working men, who studied law and history. They were especially interested in the history of the language of the German people, and they wrote several books about it, including a German grammar and a German dictionary. The study of old words and old sayings led them on to an interest in the old folk-tales that they heard in the villages and towns. They found that these old stories went far back into history and were part of the language and the customs and the wisdom of the people. They began to collect the stories and compare them and study them.

They found ordinary, uneducated people who told the stories in a simple, beautiful, direct way, just as they had heard them from their mothers and fathers. Jacob and Wilhelm wrote the stories down as nearly as possible in the way that they were spoken. They heard stories from fishermen, shepherds, miners, grandmothers, pedlars, craftsmen. They heard about magic and monsters, seven-league boots and wishing caps. They heard of vessels that never ran dry and stores of food that never became less. They heard of talking animals and fearful ogres, of beautiful princesses and poor boys who set out to seek their fortunes. They collected more than two hundred stories. Among them were the Elves and the Shoemaker, The Fisherman and His Wife, Hans in Luck, Hansel and Gretel, Rumpelstiltskin, The Three Musicians of Bremen and Tom Thumb.

In those days many people thought folk-tales were foolish and that the clever brothers were wasting their time studying such things. Jacob and Wilhelm, however, went on and on, writing quietly with their slow quill pens. They were not thinking of children at first, but in 1812 they published a book called "Nursery Household Tales". Not only did this book delight children in all the states of Germany, but it made grown-ups understand the importance of the study of folk-tales and folklore, and it led other people to collect folk-tales from many other countries. The Grimm brothers' book became one of the most popular books ever written. Three years later it was translated into English, and within a hundred and fifty years it was being read in seventy different languages.

There are still people in parts of Africa and India and in remote islands and distant jungles who have never read the stories of Perrault or the Grimm brothers. Yet they tell many of the same stories to their children. They may not be quite the same. They may have different names and slightly different plots. They are the same stories they heard from their own mothers and grandmothers. They are the stories their grandmothers heard from their great-grandmothers and great-great-grandmothers.

How is it, that so many of the stories seem to belong to so many different countries?

Is it because early man in one country thought in a manner very like early man in another country?

Is it because some of the stories have the sort of simple plots that many different people might think of at the same time?

Did the stories start in one place – India, or somewhere in the East, and then spread to other countries with travellers and traders and soldiers and slaves?

We cannot tell. We know only that the magic has come down through the ages, and that it goes on from mother to child, mother to child throughout the world – "Once upon a time –".

Johnny Appleseed

When the first settlers were moving into the lonely places of the Middle West in America, Johnny Appleseed was striding through the forests. He was a young man then, with dark hair falling past his shoulders. His clothes were shabby and his shoes were almost worn out. He carried a bag over his shoulder. In it there were apple pips – hundreds and hundreds of apple pips.

He had cut them out of apples that lay rotting under trees in other places. He had washed them out of the piles of waste at cider mills. Now he was setting out to plant his orchards in the wilderness. He was not thinking of himself, and how he might make a living by growing and selling young apple trees. He was thinking of

people who were yet to come. They would build wooden houses and make farms here. They would bring up their children to think of this land as home. They would be surprised and glad to find apple trees already growing for them.

Johnny Appleseed looked for a clearing in the forest. He cut out the bushes and undergrowth. He dug and raked the earth and put a fence of brushwood round it. Then he planted his apple pips in neat rows. He whispered a little prayer for them. Then he left them to the sun and rain and went on his way.

In a day or two he found another suitable spot, and he planted another orchard. Sometimes as he walked, he pushed apple pips into the soft mould of the forest floor in odd places. So he went on, year after year, planting new orchards and coming back from time to time to look after the growing saplings of the earlier ones.

Things happened as he had expected. People settled. They built houses, and made farms. He sold apple trees to those who could afford to pay. He gave them away to those who were poor.

Soon everyone knew him. People welcomed him for a chat or a meal. They offered him shelter for the night. He would lie by the hearth or in a shed, but he would never sleep in a bed. People would give him old clothes or shoes, and their children would listen eagerly to his stories. He would tell of his escapes from bears and rattlesnakes, and of his struggles through snow and floods.

He was always ready to help new settlers or advise old ones. He would bring back stray horses and give away little bags of apple seeds. When he had money he would hide it until he needed it. He would leave it under the roof of a cabin or push it into a hollow tree and go back for it years later. More often though, he would give it away.

He was a religious man, and he knew the secrets of the forest. He knew which plants would help sick people. He loved the animals and would not harm even the fiercest of them. Sometimes people left their old, sick horses out in the forest to die. Johnny Appleseed would look after them and take them to good pasture. Once he rescued a wolf from a trap. He nursed it back to health and it followed him for years until it died.

His food was berries and roots, and potatoes cooked in a camp fire. There was usually wild honey to be found, but Johnny Appleseed took it only when he had made sure the bees would have enough for themselves.

Year after year he went on with his work. He walked hundreds of kilometres through Ohio, Indiana, Illinois and Pennsylvania. He became older and stranger. His hair became white and longer than ever. His main garment now was usually a coffee sack with holes for his arms and head. His hat changed from time to time – a shabby felt hat, an old cloth army cap, a battered saucepan with the handle sticking out at the back. He might wear ancient shoes, or cloth bound round his feet with string. Often he was bare-footed, even in the snow.

His real name was John Chapman and he lived from 1774 to 1847. For forty-six of those years he was tramping through the country on his mission of kindness.

Even while he was still alive, many stories grew up around him, and after his death, there were even more.

In America today there are books, poems and plays about him. There are monuments and public seats to his memory. There is a Johnny Appleseed Bridge and a Johnny Appleseed park and a Johnny Appleseed school. And, of course, there are apples.

"These apples came from the seeds of apples grown on trees planted by Johnny Appleseed," people say, or:

"These can be traced back to Johnny Appleseed's orchards."

There are hundreds and hundreds of apples.

Old Cars

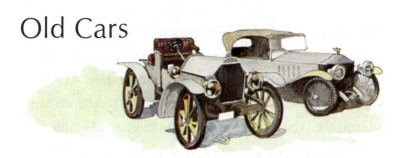

There are people who love old cars. They sometimes find them in most unlikely places. They spend months restoring them. They replace the missing parts. They clean off the rust and polish the bodywork. They try to make the cars look as handsome and shining as they did when they were new. Then, proudly, the owners drive the cars in the Veteran and Vintage car runs.

A 1905 Rolls Royce was found in the Australian bush. It had been converted to a truck and used for carrying tomatoes. It was then sold for many thousands of pounds.

A driver found an old car that had been standing in the open air for years and years. It was a 1909 Star two-seater, but it looked more like a rusty load of scrap metal. It was delivered to him in pieces on a lorry. He spent many months bringing it back to life. He was so successful that he was able to use it as an everyday car.

A 1910 Mercedes was found on a Somerset farm where it had been half buried in hay for many years. Its new owner replaced its cracked cylinder jacket and brought the car back to such good condition that he was able to get many years of happy motoring from it.

One of the proud entries in a Manchester to Blackpool Vintage car run was a 1923 Standard Warwick found filled with straw in a barn. The pushrods were missing and the engine was broken in bits. The man who bought it gave it a great deal of loving care. He had new pushrods and pistons made and gave first aid to the engine. When he first saw it, it had flat tyres and a tow bar on the back, as if it had been used for ploughing.

A 1926 Austin 20 had quite a varied life. It was built as a taxi and used for twelve years. Then a garage owner put a home-made crane on it and converted it to a breakdown truck. It worked in this way for about fifteen years and then was left out in the open at the back of the garage. There it stood rusting for ten or twelve years, until the son of the garage keeper rescued it. When he had restored it to its former glory, he entered it in many rallies in which it won cups and awards.

A 1928 Austin tourer was discovered on a farm, where it had been used for carrying pigs to market and winter feed to cattle. The man who bought it restored it to prime condition and drove it in many veteran car runs.

There must be many more ancient cars lying neglected on farms and in old barns. There must also be many keen car lovers who go on hoping and hoping to find them.

To the North

One of the most daring journeys ever taken was planned by the Norwegian explorer, Nansen. Living near Oslo, he was brought up to ski and sledge almost as soon as he could walk. He loved the long cold winters. He loved the snow and the blizzards and the frozen rivers. As he grew up, however, he realised that the snow and ice at home was nothing to the snow and ice further north, and he began to read everything he could find about the Arctic Circle and the North Pole.

What was the North Pole? Like most children, he probably imagined a flag blowing on top of a wooden pole stuck in a pile of snow. Then he began to understand that there was nothing special to see there. The only way of knowing you were there would be by using scientific instruments. But where was the North Pole? Was it on the land or was it in the sea? He thought about it and wondered about it, and he made up his mind that one day he would go and find it.

For ten months of the year, the Arctic Ocean is packed with ice. Giant ice floes and icebergs creak and crash and roar. They grind against each other and build up into hills and hummocks, sometimes as high as 15 metres above the water. Little channels of water flow between them, only to be frozen in turn until the sea is a solid mass of ice, sometimes rising into gentle hills, and sometimes rearing up in craggy caves and rocks and castles of ice.

The ice is high above the water, and thicker still beneath it, but deep down below there are currents and movement as in any sea. The currents of the Arctic Ocean drift and swirl, and slowly, slowly the great blanket of ice drifts with them. It drifts slowly, slowly, always in the same general direction, so that if the branch of a tree falls into the sea off the coast of Siberia it will be trapped in the ice and carried at last across the North Pole to Greenland. In summer, which is less than two months long, the ice breaks and separates into ice floes and icebergs again and these drift in the same way, carried by the currents across the North Pole.

Nansen studied journeys that had already been made in that part of the world. Some explorers had been northwards, but no one as yet had reached the North Pole. He himself had already crossed Greenland on skis, so he was well aware of the conditions that he would have to face. He worked out a theory of his own. It was quite different from those of other people.

He decided to sail as far north as possible and let his ship become trapped in the ice. Then it would drift, he thought, as a tree branch would drift. It would drift, slowly, slowly to the North Pole, and beyond it to

Greenland. It would take a long time – a year, two years perhaps, or even more. Of course the ship might not have the chance to drift at all, because it might be crushed by the ice, and splintered to matchwood. He would need to plan a very special ship.

So he had one built. He called it *Fram*, meaning "Forward". It was a sailing ship with three masts, but it also had an engine, driven by steam. It was very, very strong, with sides three-quarters of a metre thick. The sides sloped in such a way that the pack ice would form underneath and lift her up rather than crushing her.

With a crew of twelve men, Nansen set sail in the *Fram* during the last week of June 1893. He sailed through the Kara Sea and along the north coast of Asia.

The air grew colder, colder. The sea ice grew thicker, thicker. The sturdy *Fram* pushed and broke her way through ice floes and round towering icebergs. The struggle became harder and harder.

Then on September the twentieth, near the New Siberian Islands, the ice pressed and pressed on both sides of the *Fram*. The ice crashed and roared. The *Fram* creaked and groaned. Would Nansen's reasoning be proved wrong? Would the ship be crushed and the crew killed? It must have been an anxious day. Then the ice pressed so hard on each side of the ship that the *Fram* was lifted up on to the surface of the ice and there, instantly, it froze, trapped without hope of release.

This was what Nansen had planned, and now as he had expected, the slow drift began. The ship, of course, was packed with all kinds of stores, with food, dogs, skis, tools, materials and scientific instruments. There was plenty of work for the men to do, and they were able to go seal-hunting and even set up a camp on the ice.

Deep down in the sea, the currents swirled and drifted. Slowly, slowly, the great blanket of ice drifted with them. Slowly, slowly the *Fram*, the whole camp, and all the men and dogs drifted too.

Nansen was delighted. He planned the men's work and play so that they scarcely ever became bored. They took the *Fram*'s engine apart, oiled it, and put it carefully away. They made tools, more scientific instruments, sledges, dog harnesses, tents, sleeping bags and kayaks. The kayaks were skin boats of Eskimo type, but shorter and wider. If two were lashed together they were big enough to carry dogs and stores and two or three sledges. For recreation, there were games on the ice, or musical evenings, or books to read.

There were also polar bears to watch, and on two occasions a bear climbed on to the *Fram* at night, and stole an unfortunate dog. Nansen, who was quite an artist, drew many charming pictures of bears. He wrote descriptions of the day's activities, and he described in wonder the beauty of the polar days, and the colours of the polar nights, when the sky would change from blue and green to mauve and purple, with waves of light and bands of moving colour – yellow and red and pink and shining silver.

So the *Fram* drifted for a year, two years. It drifted in a world of white where sometimes the ice gleamed

cold and green and sometimes was touched with pink and blue and violet. The ice under the *Fram* was nine metres thick and there were often mists and blizzards and swirling snowfalls. All the time, the men were learning more and more about the cold Arctic sea. They drifted nearer and nearer to the North Pole. Everything seemed to be going well.

Then, in March 1895 they realised that they were going to miss the North Pole after all. They were drifting now too far out of line. They could not in any way fight the drift or change their course.

Nansen proposed that one man should join him and that they should leave the *Fram* and do the rest of the journey on skis.

"We will ski and walk across the frozen sea," he explained, "and we will take some of the dogs to pull the sledges."

It was a most daring plan, and every one of the men hoped *he* would be the one to go. Nansen chose Johansen, a strong, tough, brave member of the crew. They packed the three sledges with food for a hundred days. They also took two kayaks, a number of scientific instruments, a couple of guns, a small tent and some of the dogs. On March the fourteenth they said goodbye to the rest of the men and they set off across the snow-covered ice of the Arctic Ocean. The *Fram* drifted slowly onwards and was quickly lost to sight in mist.

At first the way for Nansen and Johansen was not too difficult, but after a few days it became harder and harder. The cold was so bitter that Nansen and Johansen found that their clothes froze to their bodies and tore their skin until it was sore and bleeding. The cold was so bitter that even the mercury froze in the thermometers. You might think that sledges would skim easily over the ice, but ice and snow had often been frozen into high ridges and small hills. The men would often have to help the dogs to drag the sledges over the worst places. Sometimes the dogs' traces became tangled. The dogs themselves became much weaker, and the men seemed to come to the end of their strength again and again. After the day's march and the setting up of the tent at evening, they would often be so tired that they would fall asleep with food half-way to their mouths.

Nearly a month later, Nansen made one of the hardest decisions of his life. He realised that, in spite of all their hard work and determination, he and Johansen were unlikely to reach the Pole. They had gone as far north as they were likely to get on foot. They had gone nearer to the North Pole than anyone else before them, but now they knew that for them, it was going to be an impossible dream. If they wished to remain alive, the only thing to do was to turn back, and this they did. They hoped to go south and reach Spitzbergen. They hoped to meet the *Fram* again somewhere on her homeward way. They left the flag of Norway standing on the ice, and for a few days they made good progress, ski-ing over the frozen sea, with the dogs hauling the sledges.

Summer came, with the sun shining day and night. This was a welcome sight for it meant that the cold was no longer so intense. At the same time it was unwelcome because the firm fields of ice began to melt and turn into slush. Sledging and ski-ing became almost impossible. Yet using the kayaks was impossible too. The tragedy of dogs in the Arctic followed the usual pattern. There was little food for them. They became weaker and weaker. There was nothing that Nansen and Johansen could do but to kill them one by one to provide food for the others. The men were very sad about this, but it had to be done.

Now they had to struggle against rain and snow showers but gradually the ice was breaking up. Ice floes were separating and floating apart. Little channels were opening up in the sea. The men were able to use the kayaks from time to time, and now and then to kill a seal or a bear for food.

So they continued, sometimes drifting or rowing the kayaks, sometimes marching on the ice floes. One day Johansen was on an ice floe, and Nansen was just dragging his kayak up to join him, when he heard a shout. There was Johansen lying on the ground with a great polar bear on top of him. Johansen had his hand against the bear's throat, trying desperately to push it away.

Nansen, struggling with his slipping kayak, managed to get hold of his gun. He fired. For one dreadful moment Johansen's life was in the balance. Then Nansen's bullet found its mark, and the bear tottered and fell dead.

The journey on the frozen sea had lasted several months, but now ice was rapidly turning to water so that early in August the men were able to use the kayaks most of the time. To make it easier, they tied them together and fixed the sledges across them. Then they put up a sail and drifted through the misty days until, on August the fifteenth, they landed on an island off the coast of Franz Josef Land. It was two years since they had stood on land, and now they stretched their weary bodies on the ground and gazed thankfully at patches of moss and bright tufts of Arctic wild flowers – saxifrage and poppies. They saw small bubbling streams, and seabirds that wheeled and cried above them.

This, however, was not the end of the journey and the hardships. This was not Spitzbergen, or even inhabited land. Winter was closing in again and the sea was freezing once more so that there could be no further progress till the spring. They sailed a little further along the coast and then landed again and built themselves a hut. They used a runner from one of the sledges and the shoulder bone of a walrus to pull away stones at the foot of a cliff. They built the hut of stones, pressed together with snow and moss and roofed with walrus hide. Nansen could not stand quite upright in it and the floor measured three metres by one and three-quarters. Food was no longer a problem, for not only were there many seabirds, but there were seals and walrus and bears to hunt. Soon there was a pile of warm bear skins to use as mattresses under the sleeping bags, and there was a large store of frozen bear meat to last through the winter.

Winter must have seemed very long to the two men – nine cold months without a glimpse of the sun. The bears hibernated and the birds flew away. The sea froze and the world was still and white, with snow and mist swirling outside the hut, so that there was scarcely ever the chance even to take a walk. There was nothing to do except cook and eat bear meat and bear soup, and then write and sleep and dream of home and of washing in warm water and soap and eating delicious dinners. All the same, Nansen and Johansen kept in good health and good spirits.

In May 1896 spring came again. Once more the sea ice began to crack and break. Ice floes separated and floated apart. Little channels opened up in the sea, and an unfortunate bear crept out of hibernation in time to be shot and provide fresh meat. Once more Nansen and Johansen lashed the kayaks together, put up a sail and took to the water. They progressed as before, sailing round and between the ice floes, hoping still to reach Spitzbergen.

One day they landed on an ice floe to consider the next part of the voyage. They pulled the kayaks out of the water and tied them to a jagged point of ice. A little later, to their horror, they saw that the boats had slipped off the ice floe and were floating away with the sledges and all the stores. If the kayaks were lost, there would be no chance at all of survival.

Nansen did not hesitate. He dived into the water at once and swam after them. He could not have lived for many minutes in that freezing sea, but it must have seemed a very long time to him before he caught hold of the kayaks, clambered aboard and rowed them back to the ice floe. Johansen helped Nansen on to the ice. Nansen was shivering and his teeth were chattering noisily. Johansen pushed him into a sleeping bag and covered him with the tent, the sail and everything else that he could find, and Nansen fell asleep.

. . . . . .

A month later the men landed again, this time on Franz Josef Land. Soon afterwards, on June the seventeenth, Nansen stood still, listening to the seabirds. There were thousands of them, wheeling and circling overhead, shrieking and crying and calling. Suddenly he heard another noise – quite a different one. It sounded like the barking of a dog, but of course it could not be.

"Johansen," he called. "There's a dog barking! Listen!"

Johansen thought Nansen's mind must be wandering. What dog would be barking in this desolate place? But Nansen heard it again, and in a moment he was following tracks, not of one dog, but of many. They led to a large camp, belonging to Frederick Jackson, an English explorer who had also hoped to reach the Pole. Nansen told him it was in the sea and could be reached only in winter over the ice.

It was three years since Nansen and Johansen had been in touch with the world. Now Jackson gave them news of Norway, and letters from their families. A little later his ship called to take them all back to Norway, and on that voyage they met the *Fram* also on its way back.

Nansen and Johansen joined their old ship and entered the port at Oslo where thousands of people had gathered to cheer and wave and welcome them home as heroes.

. . . .

Much more could be told of Nansen – how he helped to make Norway free of Sweden – how he worked for world peace in the League of Nations – how he raised £250 000 in six weeks to feed ten million starving Russians – how he helped refugees of many countries, and produced the "Nansen passport" for stateless people – how he was given the Nobel prize for his work for humanity. He had to attend banquets and make speeches and give lectures. So many people wanted to see him and listen to him, that often he found himself longing for the peace and quiet beauty of the Arctic.

Canals

There are many canals in Britain – long ones, short ones, wide ones, narrow ones. They join one town with another town, or one river with another river. They run through quiet fields where trees cast their shadows on the water. They run beside streets of houses or through long, black tunnels.

Once they were very busy, with boats carrying people, and barges carrying coal and grain, iron and cotton, timber and gravel. The tow paths echoed with the sound of horses going clip clop, clip clop, as they pulled the barges slowly along. In those days most of the business and trade of the whole country was carried on up and down the canals.

Most of the canals were built or planned by James Brindley. He was a very ordinary man with rather rough manners and speech, and he could scarcely read or write. Yet as a self-taught engineer he was brilliant. He had a special understanding of the lie of the land. He could tell, just by looking round, which was the best place to put a canal. He did not draw plans or diagrams. He did not write down figures or measurements. He worked out everything in his head.

The first canal he made was for the Duke of Bridgewater, who lived in the north of England. He had coal on his land, and he wanted to sell it to people in Manchester, a distance of more than sixteen kilometres. The year was 1759 and at that time the roads were very bad indeed. They were rough and muddy and full of holes and ruts. In wet weather, some of the ruts were so deep that you could have swum in them, or more likely, drowned in them. Rivers, too, were not always very good for transport purposes. They often flooded or flowed too fast, or they were too shallow or not wide enough.

The Duke of Bridgewater had seen canals in Europe, and he thought a canal would solve his problem. So he paid James Brindley to make it for him. The country people must have gazed in amazement as the channel for the canal was dug, and they heard that a man was

actually *making* a river. They must have been even more amazed to see what Brindley did when his canal reached the River Irwell. He built a stone bridge with three arches so that the canal could flow along it in a trough, and cross over the river below. This seemed like one of the wonders of the world, for people could see barges being pulled along by horses on top of the bridge. It looked as if there were boats in the sky.

This was the beginning of the canal age in Britain. More and more of them were built, making a network of waterways across the countryside. When hills stood in the way, long tunnels were made through them, or locks were built to make it possible for boats to travel up rising land, or down sloping fields.

A lock was made by enclosing a section of the canal, just a little bit longer than any of the boats that used it. Walls were built of wood, brick or stone (later steel and concrete) making a sort of open box, with a pair of gates at each end. The gates at the higher end closed by meeting at an angle like the head of an arrow. This was to help them withstand the pressure of the water. When they were open they fitted back into the sides of the box.

A boat going up the canal would enter the lock, and the gates at both ends would be closed. Water would then be let in slowly through sluices in the sides or in the gates. The water level in the box would rise, and the boat would rise with it, until it was level with the water in the higher part of the canal. The upper gates would then be opened and the boat would continue on

its way. It was rather like taking a lift from one floor to a higher one.

If the slope were very long, a whole series of locks were built, like a staircase of lifts. One of the longest of these flights of locks is near Devizes, where there are twenty-nine.

The men who worked on the barges (or narrow boats as they were called) took several days over each journey. It was a lonely way to live, month after month, so, soon they began to take their wives and children with them. The narrow boats then became family homes, and the cargo was pulled along on the barge or barges behind.

The front boat was known as the butty. It was now fitted up with bunk-beds and a place to cook and eat meals. The women soon put lace curtains at the small cabin windows and made everything as comfortable as they could. It became the fashion to decorate the barges with gay pictures of castles and roses. They were painted on the doors and inside the cabins, and on the wooden water cans, and often along the sides of the barges too. No one really knows how this idea started, but even today there are still castles and roses to be seen.

The families who lived on the narrow boats became almost a race on their own, with their own special words and signs and their own special way of life. The father would steer most of the time. Another man, or one of the boys of the family, would lead the horses along the tow path beside the canal. The mother would cook the meals, and sometimes take a turn at the steering. The baby would have a rope tied round its waist so that it could not crawl to the edge and fall off. The children would scramble in and out of the cabin, and play their games, and shout their greetings to children in other narrow boats passing by. Festoons of washing would wave in the breeze above the deck, and a little trail of ripples would follow along in the water behind.

There would be lock gates to open and shut, and the excitement of feeling the boat rising or sinking to a different level of water. There would be tunnels to go through. These were often long and black and frightening. The mother, or one of the bigger children, would jump ashore and unfasten the horses and lead them along the path beside the canal, while the father guided the boat into the darkness of the tunnel. He would lie down and work his way through by pressing his feet against the wall at the side. The tunnel would smell damp and musty, and drops of ice-cold water would drip from the roof. Strange noises would echo and resound from side to side – the father's heavy breathing, the baby's cry, the drip, drip, drip from the roof, the lapping of the water against the sides of the narrow boat. All these would sound loud and eerie and unreal.

Then at last a tiny glimmer of light would appear in the distance. It would grow bigger and bigger, and the tunnel would come at last to an end. The father and family would blink in the daylight again and thankfully breathe deeply of the clean fresh air.

The canals were really the life-line of trading for about eighty years, and by 1840 they stretched for 6840 kilometres. Then the railways came. The new invention pushed out the old. Trains could carry heavier loads than barges. Trains were faster than narrow boats. A journey that would take several days on a canal, could be done in a few hours by railway. Speed became the important thing. Goods were transported in railway wagons now, and many of the narrow boats went out of business. In a short time, only about a quarter of the canals were being used.

There are still a small number of narrow boats at work, but in these days they are motor driven. They have often been passed down from father to son, but the horses have gone long ago. There are still some families who live in the old way, chugging up and down the canals, with their washing waving in the breeze above the deck, and their cabins and water jugs still decorated with pictures of castles and roses.

Many of the canals, however, are lying sad and deserted. Some are empty and dry and crumbling away.

Some are overgrown with reeds and rushes and young trees and tangled weeds. Some are blocked with rubbish – old mattresses and battered tins, broken glass and rusty iron bedsteads. In others the water lies dark and murky. Gone are the horses plodding along the banks. Gone are the narrow boats and their families. Gone is a whole way of life. The canals are lonely and silent and forgotten.

But for a few, there is hope. They are being cleared and cleaned and opened for holiday use. Parents can take their families out on them in rowing boats or teach their children how to sail. People can hire a cabin cruiser or even a narrow boat and drift along for a week or more.

There is an idea too, that we ought to return a lot of our transport to the canals. Roads become more and more crowded. Long-distance lorries become bigger and bigger and more heavily laden. Railways become more and more expensive to run. There is quite a lot to be said for a narrow boat pulling its load slowly along a canal, far away from motorways and speed and traffic jams.